HORSE & PONY BREEDS

HORSE & PONY BREEDS

BARNES & NOBLE BOOKS

NEW YORK

This edition published by Barnes & Noble, Inc.,
by arrangement with Book Sales, Inc.

2004 Barnes & Noble Books

This edition produced for sales in the U.S.A., its
territories, and dependencies only.

M 10 9 8 7 6 5 4 3 2 1

ISBN 0-7607-6227-9

This book was designed and produced by
Quintet Publishing Limited
6 Blundell Street
London N7 9BH

Designed and Edited by Q2A Solutions

Publisher: Ian Castello-Cortés
Associate Publisher: Laura Price
Creative Director: Richard Dewing

Art Director: Roland Codd
Project Editors: Jenny Doubt, Catherine Osborne

Manufactured in Singapore by Pica Digital Pte Ltd
Printed in Singapore by Star Standard Industries (Pte) Ltd.

The material used in this publication previously appeared in
The Kingdom of the Horse by Caroline Davis (ed.), *Illustrated
Encyclopedia of Horse Breeds* by Susan McBane, and *Horse and
Pony Breeds* by Caroline Ball.

Contents

Ideal Conformation

Conformation is a horse's make and shape, which depends on its skeleton. Despite a great variety of conformation, a common basic blueprint of shape exists within each breed and type.

The most important factor overall is balance. The lines of the body should flow and have a pleasing symmetry.

Horses with good conformation can be of quite different shapes. The Thoroughbred, at one extreme, has a light, sleek frame, long legs in relation to its trunk, a sloped shoulder for speed, and a long neck. The heavy draft horse, at the other end of the spectrum, has a much deeper trunk and shorter legs in proportion to its height, an "upright" shoulder, a shorter, thicker neck, and a bigger head. Its limbs are generally much thicker than those of the Thoroughbred.

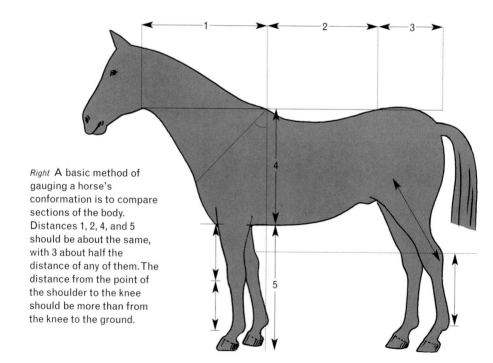

Right **A** basic method of gauging a horse's conformation is to compare sections of the body. Distances 1, 2, 4, and 5 should be about the same, with 3 about half the distance of any of them. The distance from the point of the shoulder to the knee should be more than from the knee to the ground.

POINTS OF THE HORSE

1 Hoof Wall	10 Point of Shoulder	19 Loins
2 Pastern	11 Shoulder	20 Croup
3 Cannon	12 Throat	21 Stifle
4 Knee	13 Poll	22 Tail
5 Flank	14 Forelock	23 Dock
6 Forearm	15 Mane	24 Hock
7 Girth	16 Crest	25 Tendons
8 Point of Elbow	17 Withers	26 Fetlock
9 Breast	18 Back	27 Heel

Measuring a Horse

A horse or pony is traditionally measured in "hands" (hh) and inches — each hand being 4 inches (10 cm), the approximate width of a man's hand. For example, an animal measuring 58 inches from the ground to its wither would be 14.2 hh (14 hands and two inches high). Horses and ponies are measured from the highest point of the withers down to the ground in a perpendicular line. This measurement is derived from when people measured their animals by placing their hands (four inches being the approximate width across a man's knuckles) sideways, going up from the ground to the highest point of the withers.

Nowadays, measuring sticks are calibrated in hands and inches. The animal is stood on level ground with forelegs together and the stick placed next to its shoulder with the arm touching the top of its withers.

In pure breeds one can be fairly certain, to an inch or so, what height a foal is likely to mature to, becuase they are consistent in height. However, with cross-breeds, it is difficult to ascertain what height the animal will grow to unless a mating between a particular mare and a stallion had been carried out before, and the resulting offspring's height had been recorded at birth.

Gradually, metric measurements are starting to replace traditional hand measuring techniques, for example a pony measuring 13.2hh (54 inches) is approximately 137 cm high. An equine is considered a pony if it measures 14.2hh and under, whereas a horse measures over 14.2hh.

Left Horses are measured from the highest point of the withers.

THE HORSE'S GAITS

A horse's action is the way in which it moves. Whatever the type of horse, a straight, true action is essential, with the hindlegs following exactly the same plane as the forelegs. When a horse with a good action is approaching you head-on, its hindlegs should be barely visible to your eye. A horse with good action will move from its shoulders and not just the elbows, placing the forehoofs down well under the head.

WALK This is the slowest gait. The sequence for walk may be in a regular, four-beat rhythm. There is no moment of suspension in walk.

TROT An active, two-beat gait, the legs moving in diagonal pairs, the horse springing from one pair to another, with a moment of suspension when the horse has all four feet off the ground.

CANTER This is a three-beat gait, with a moment of suspension at the end of each stride.

GALLOP A very fast four-beat gait, which is a natural extension of the canter.

Coat Colors and Markings

Coat colors and markings developed over millions of years in order to give horses the best possible camouflage for the area in which they lived. The more a coat resembled its background, the less likely the horse was to be spotted by a predator. One of the most primitive colors is dun (a yellow beige), with black points (the points being the mane, forelock, tail, and lower legs). In a woodland background, or on plains where by no means everything is a lush green, duns are extremely well camouflaged. The horse colors which are abundant today, however, are the result of domesticated breeding, and bear no relation to camouflage.

There are also many age-old stories of good and bad colors in horses. Chestnut horses are supposedly hot-tempered, while black ones are said to be ill-tempered and lacking in stamina. Bays and browns are believed to be dependable. In reality, however, color has no bearing whatsoever on a horse's temperament or performance.

MARKINGS

Markings are areas of white on the body, limbs, and head of a horse. The terms used to describe them have been officially laid down by the various breeding authorities. On the body these are zebra marks and whorls (patterns of hairs around a small central point). Markings on the leg are called either "socks" or "stockings."

Left This Sumba Pony shows a dark dorsal, eel stripe, or list, going all the way down his spine from poll to tail.

FACIAL MARKINGS

Facial markings are an important means of identification. Some common markings are shown below. Where a star occurs, the position, size, and shape should be noted; whereas a stripe should be classed as "narrow" or "broad."

White Face

Snip

Blaze

Star

Stripe

WHITE FACE Forehead, eyes, nose, and parts of the muzzle are white.
SNIP Small white line running into or around the nostril.
BLAZE Broad white line from eyes to the muzzle.
STAR Small white patch on forehead.
STRIPE White line down the face.

COLORS

Compared to his primitive ancestors, the domesticated horse has a wide variety of coat colors and markings. Color variations came about because of the interbreeding of primitive types. The colors of primitive ancestors comprised variations ranging from yellow to uniform gray, and medium to dark brown. Shadings such as lighter underparts, muzzles, and eye area also occurred, along with a dorsal list or eel stripe down the back, and zebra markings on the legs.

Prehistoric paintings and carvings reveal that mottled, spotted, and sometimes striped horses were well known to prehistoric man. In fact, spotted and mottled horses were popular in Europe until about a couple of hundred years ago, and crossed the Atlantic with the conquistadors. These horses normally have vertically striped hoofs.

Color is carried by a pigment in the skin called melanin; the color depends on the amount and type of melanin present. Breeding for color is not always easy because although color is determined by genes, throwbacks and variations often occur.

THE ALBINO HORSE

White markings are areas with no pigment, and do not appear to have existed in primitive and early strains. Albino horses have white coats, pink skin, and red eyes. The blood that circulates through colorless skin gives their skin a pink hue. Furthermore, because they lack melanin, they are much more susceptible to the weather than other horses.

Left The skin of albinos is often susceptible to diseases like mud fever, rain rash, and sunburn. These conditions, however, are controllable with good management.

DIFFERENT SHADES

Different shades and varieties exist within each color category. Some of the most common ones are shown below. If there is any doubt about the color of a horse, it is decided by the color of the points — the muzzle, tips of the ears, mane and tail, and lower part of the legs.

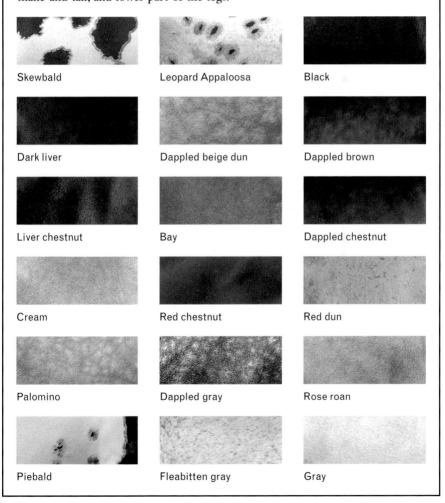

Skewbald

Leopard Appaloosa

Black

Dark liver

Dappled beige dun

Dappled brown

Liver chestnut

Bay

Dappled chestnut

Cream

Red chestnut

Red dun

Palomino

Dappled gray

Rose roan

Piebald

Fleabitten gray

Gray

Understanding Your Horse

Horses and ponies are by nature highly strung and reactive, a phenomenon which can be explained by their evolutionary process. Horses evolved as prey animals, and the instinct to run at the first sign of danger has been little changed by 5,000 years of domestication. Even the most obedient police horse will succumb to its instinct to run when frightened. This means that riders must learn to be calm and quiet around horses.

THE HERD INSTINCT

Horses live in herds as a form of defense. Within the herd there is a strict but flexible hierarchy, although animals also form strong individual bonds with each other. Different animals may be dominant in different facets of herd life. For example, one individual may be dominant over grazing, another over shelter. Fighting in established herds is rare. Not all horses crave close company, but they are usually friendly and tolerant toward each other and even toward those of other species.

LEARNING EXPERIENCES

Horses learn quickly, and rarely forget an experience, though the same property which allows the horse to learn can also have a negative result.

Although horses can get over a bad experience, such as a traffic accident or a bad fall, many never completely recover. Trainers must therefore be sure not to hurt or frighten a horse that is doing its best to cooperate; otherwise, the animal will associate training with frustration, and will be unable to learn.

Above Horses will run in a pack like this when frightened. They will normally only turn and fight when they have no escape route, or must stand their ground.

Left Mutual scratching is a benefit enjoyed by those horses kept in groups; alone, a horse would need to find a tree or fence to alleviate an itch in inaccessible places.

BREAKING IN USING A LUNGE REIN

Using a lunge rein is a common way to "break in" or initially train horses in English-type equitation. The trainer stands with the horse on a long (lunge) rein, and works the horse mainly in circles around him or her.

At first the youngster is led with the trainer, and maybe an assistant who stands close to it and teaches it basic commands such as "walk," "trot," "canter," and "whoa" for stop.

Gradually, the trainer moves farther and farther away from the horse as it becomes used to the various commands. Lunging, as it is called, teaches the horse to obey the voice, and is a useful method of early training. However, it should not be overdone, as working in circles can be very hard work, particularly for young animals.

EQUINE COMMUNICATION

Horses communicate mainly through body language and facial expressions. They also use their voices. Interest is shown by ears pricked toward the interesting object or person, alert eyes, head held high if the object is distant or more flexed inward if it is near, and nostrils flared and perhaps quivering if the horse is near enough to smell the object or person.

Fear is shown by the ears being directed toward the object. The eyes will look wide and alarmed, the nostrils wide open, and the skin will be tightly drawn across the face.

The attitude of "flehmen" is when a horse is closely examining an odor. It breathes in the smell, raises its head and turns its upper lip up to hold the smell in its air passages where the sensory Jacobsen's organ analyzes the odor.

Stallions herd their mares and offspring with a "snaking" motion. The head and neck are outstretched and held low as he goes along, usually at a trot, snaking his head and neck from side to side.

Left In most countries, horses are initially trained on long reins like the one depicted, or on single reins (lunge or longe).

REACTING TO A THREAT

Anger, dislike, or threat toward a particular individual is shown by outstretched head, flat ears, angry eyes, and drawn back and wrinkled nostrils. In the wild, this stance warns off intruders and those who stray into the horse's personal space. The teeth may also be bared and ready to bite or warn.

A sign of submission in youngsters is the outstretched head held fairly low, with the front teeth gently snapped repeatedly together. This is called "mouthing." The illustrations below demonstrate these various reactions to a threat.

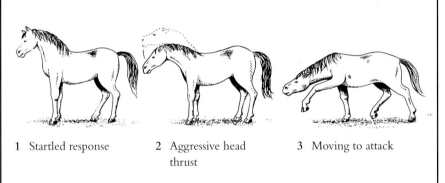

1 Startled response

2 Aggressive head thrust

3 Moving to attack

4 "Bottoms up" action — warning

5 Fighting

Good Horse Management

The modern horse is a highly specialized grazing and running animal, perfectly fitted for a life on grassy plains. Early in its evolution, the horse's ancestors lived in swampy forests and browsed leaves from trees. Horses will still browse, but most prefer grazing.

EATING LIKE A HORSE

As a large animal, the horse requires a lot of food. It must eat a lot of grass to stay healthy, and so, must eat most of the time. Grass consists of roughage, water, and nutrients, the proportion of which varies with the season. Wild horses will eat for about 15 — 18 hours a day, while domesticated horses in stables should be provided with a constant supply of food, usually hay. A horse provided with an erratic food supply will become stressed, which can cause colic — a potentially life-

threatening digestive disturbance. Feeding a horse with small but regular portions is called "trickle feeding."

When horses are worked harder than they would work themselves, they need to be provided with more concentrated nourishment. Oats, corn, barley, and branded concentrated foods are all popular supplements. However, these are not natural foodstuffs, and can cause digestive problems if administered in large quantities.

KEEP ON MOVING

The natural lifestyle of a horse is almost constant walking, and eating as it goes. Domestic horses should be allowed to mimic this as far as possible, even if they are stabled. Two hours exercise a day, mostly walking with some trotting and perhaps cantering, is the minimum requirement to keep most stabled horses healthy and happy.

FEEDING FOR FITNESS

Gradually increasing exercise, coupled with careful feeding, will produce a fit horse. In the past, a horse's fibrous feed was reduced in favor of energy-giving grains for fitness. This is now considered wrong, because horses need nutritious fiber. Even the hardest working horses should not have its hay ration cut to less than 50% of its daily feed allowance.

Above Movement is essential to the horse for health, mental contentment, and satisfaction. Most horses love exercise.

Far Left The modern horse is a grazing and running animal, perfectly fitted for a life on grassy plains. Early in its evolution, the horse's ancestors lived in swampy forests and browsed leaves from trees. Although horses will still browse, most prefer grazing.

STRONG AS A HORSE

Horses are strong, athletic animals, and can work harder than most other animals and humans. A working horse, however, must be fit to avoid injury. Fitness can be increased by building up the severity and duration of exercise. The body then reacts to the increasing stress by strengthening itself to cope with the same amount of work next time it is required.

If a horse is unfit (soft), it will take six weeks of walking, trotting, and short canters to get fit for lessons and schooling, half a day's hunting, or pleasure riding. Another six weeks of increasing work will make it fit for most jobs, and a full 16-week program, including specialized training for particular disciplines, will have the horse fit for high-level competition, eventing, endurance rides, or races.

A LITTLE EXTRA HELP

A preventive medicine program can be devised by a vet. It should cover essentials such as de-worming, vaccinations, dental treatment, and blood profiles to check on health and fitness, as well as an annual veterinary medical, which is important before starting a fitness regime.

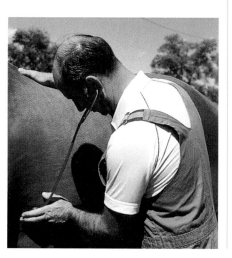

Above The farm horse came into its own in the eighteenth and nineteenth centuries.

Left A veterinary surgeon can help devise a preventive medicine program for your horse to help you keep him in good health.

SHOEING

Most working horses need shoes to prevent footsores and excessive wear of the feet. Most shoes are made of mild steel, and not iron, as is popularly believed. Aluminum shoes (plates) are normally used for racing because they are very light.

Shoeing is hard, dirty, and dangerous work. The blacksmith must first remove the old shoes and trim the excess horn, which will have grown since the last time the horse was shod. He then shapes and balances the feet, adjusts new shoes to fit, and affixes them to the horse.

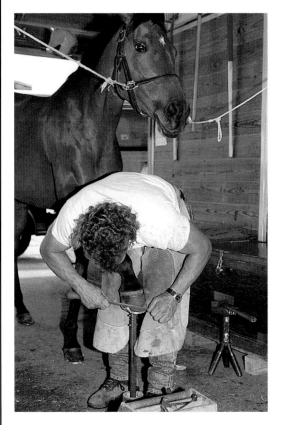

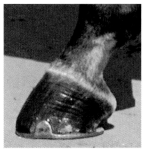

Below Strong horn and well-shaped feet are important features in any breed. However, most working horses still need the protection of properly made and fitted shoes.

Creating Horse Breeds

Horse breeds are created by breeders who first select horses whose characteristics are desirable, and then mate them together. With this type of selective breeding, the members of the group will have identical, recognizable characteristics usually within about five generations. Once the inheritance of characteristics can be reliably predicted in a reasonable number of matings, the group is said to be "breeding true." Indeed, until a group of animals does breed true, it cannot be correctly described as a "breed." Many of the newer types of horses such as the Palomino have been designated as breeds, but are not yet true breeds.

A modern breed is an artificial mating group selected by man and usually descendant from a common ancestor. The members of a breed are sufficiently alike genetically, as well as in appearance and behavior. This distinguishes them from all other members of the species, and ensures that offspring bear strong resemblance.

Below The General Stud Book is the registry for the Thoroughbred breed.

Above The ability to pass on characteristics to offspring is called "prepotency" by breeders.

Modern breeds are usually managed by a breed society which maintains a stud book. The stud book is a record of animals belonging to the breed, and their pedigrees. The breed society decides which animals shall be admitted to the stud book and sets the standards for inclusion — standards include height, color, markings, health, conformation, and performance. Animals may not be admitted to the stud book if they do not meet the requirements, even if their parents are fully registered in the stud book. Some breed societies insist on having horses blood-typed for authentication and identification purposes. Different breed societies have different criteria.

A type of horse or pony is defined as a group of animals which look alike. They may not be genetically related, and may or may not be part of any particular breed. They are usually defined by purpose or by color; for example, Hack, Hunter, and Polo Pony.

HOW TO ACHIEVE
A CERTAIN BREED

When people want to create a breed of horse for a certain purpose, either for an activity or particular appearance, they mate together mares and stallions which possess at least some of the desirable characteristics.

Sometimes an animal is strongly dominant in breeding and passes to its offspring most of its own characteristics, good and bad. Such animals are good for breeding as they reliably produce offspring like themselves. Dominant (called "prepotent") animals can be mares or stallions, but dominant stallions have more influence on a breed.

For example, to produce good trotting horses, such as the Standardbred, the breeder mates together animals which are good at trotting; to create a breed for pulling heavy loads, animals which are heavy and very strong are mated together.

The modern competition warmblood was created initially by continental European nations to have an elastic scopy gait and a powerful jump — their aim was to produce a world-class dressage and show jumping horse.

Left By selectively breeding individual horses, man can promote characteristics such as strength and agility.

STANDARDBRED

One of the fastest harness-racing horses in the world, the Standardbred is an exceptional breed. It was developed in North America during the eighteenth century, and almost all can be traced back to four stallions sired by the exceptional Thoroughbred trotter called Messanger. Its ancestry contains a variety of strong and agile breeds. The Norfolk Roadster and Hackney both have superior trotting ability and this has been passed onto the Standardbred. "Naturalized" North American types and the Morgan passed on quality trotting gaits, whereas the Thoroughbred gave the Standardbred its strength, courage, and speed.

Its name comes from the standard for trotting which was laid down by the American Trotting Register in 1879. Trotters had to attain a time of 2 minutes 30 seconds over 1 mile (1.6 km) and pacers a time of 2 minutes 25 seconds.

North America

Quarter Horse
Saddlebred
Appaloosa
Chincoteague
Pony of the Americas
Canadian Cutting Horse
Rocky Mountain Pony
Mustang
Morgan
Tennesee Walking Horse
American Shetland
Standardbred
Missouri Fox Trotter
Palomino
Pinto

Quarter Horse

The story of the Quarter Horse mirrors that of the United States itself, beginning with the Spanish horses brought to North America by Spanish explorers in the sixteenth century, some of which made their way into the care of Native Americans. These horses were later crossed with the English-bred horses brought to America by early settlers along the east coast. The resulting progeny were valued for their ability to run quarter-mile races in the blink of an eye. As the early Americans' racing passions became dominated by the longer-distance Thoroughbreds, the Quarter Horse followed westward-bound pioneers to a new territory, where it would eventually become considered a premier cow horse.

Above Although primarily developed as a short-distance racehorse, the Quarter Horse is as well known for its skills in Western riding disciplines.

CHARACTER Noted for their extremely fast standing starts, great speed over short distances, and cow sense, Quarter Horses are also known to be docile and willing, while being lively and energetic at the same time. Their build facilitates a free, straight stride, and exceptionally nimble action.

PHYSIQUE Exceptionally muscular and big-boned, particularly in the shoulders, hindquarters, and thighs; hard, tough legs and feet; muscular, wide, deep, and rounded quarters with a fairly low-set tail; stifles and thighs often wider than the hips; moderately long and well-pricked ears; short and broad head; wide forehead; large, calm, yet alert, eyes; short, straight, and strong back running into broad, muscular loins; muscular, rather straight neck carried fairly low; small and "tight" muzzle; large, mobile nostrils to facilitate rapid air exchange.

FEATURES Extremely versatile; strong; tough; hardy.

COLOR The Quarter Horse comes in all solid colors. There are variations of dun and roan-based colors; sorrel and chestnut are classic.

USES Riding; driving; working cattle; racing.

HEIGHT Larger than in the past: between 15hh and 16hh.

ANCESTRY

Based on the Iberian horse, various European and Oriental genes were mixed into the breed during colonial days, with later additions of Thoroughbred blood.

Below The Quarter Horse is small-muzzled, the head is short and broad, and carried on a muscular; fairly straight neck.

Saddlebred

The Saddlebred is one of the most glamorous, lovable, and indeed, loving horses. Apart from its supremely stylish appearance and spirited nature, it has one of the kindest temperaments of any horse.

An American original, the Saddlebred is a specially gaited breed that was developed as an obedient, enduring working horse to serve plantation workers of the southern United States (principally Kentucky, where its forerunner was called the Kentucky Saddler). Plantation owners had sought to produce a horse that could both be ridden along the primitive trails of newly developed rural areas, while looking stylish in harness.

The horse also had to be extremely comfortable for hours under saddle, and also fast, but the gallop was not a practical gait for its job, so two other gaits were developed in addition to walk, trot, and canter.

These horses are said to be "three-gaited" and "five-gaited": the three-gaited horses show the walk, trot, and canter, and the five-gaited horses show the "slow gait" and the "rack." Very high, exaggerated action is encouraged by keeping the feet very long, by fitting heavy shoes, and by training.

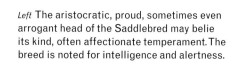

Left The aristocratic, proud, sometimes even arrogant head of the Saddlebred may belie its kind, often affectionate temperament. The breed is noted for intelligence and alertness.

Above The Saddlebred appearance is very distinct, with its long legs, high head, and artificially nicked and set tail. The breed is produced mainly for the showring.

ANCESTRY

Distant ancestors include trotting and pacing breeds from England and Europe. The Narragansett Pacer (developed on Rhode Island in the seventeenth century), the Canadian Pacer, the Morgan, and the Thoroughbred were also used. Blended together, they produced a truly distinctive, quality riding horse.

CHARACTER The Saddlebred is fiery, graceful, spirited, and proud, yet so gentle it can be handled and ridden by children.

PHYSIQUE Refined yet athletic; long neck; sloping shoulders; strong and level back; wide, powerful loins and flat quarters with a naturally high-set tail; fine, tough, and well-muscled legs; prominent withers; lovely head with expressive eyes; fine, pointed ears.

COLOR All solid colors, including palomino; occasionally roan. Some white may be seen on head and lower legs. Very fine, silky coat and mane hair.

USES Driving; competition; riding.

HEIGHT 15hh to 16.1hh.

Appaloosa

The Appaloosa actually began as the guarded treasure of the Nez Percé Indian tribe in the northwestern United States. The defining moment in the tribe's relationship with the Appaloosa occurred when the tribe was targeted for relocation by the United States Cavalry in the late 1800s. The Nez Percé made a legendary trek in excess of 1,000 miles into Canada. Though they failed in their escape, they never could have made it as far as they did without their devoted Appaloosas.

Though the Appaloosa, too, was targeted for destruction for its Native American links, the breed prevailed, and is one of the most popular breeds in the United States, today.

Left Appaloosas are of compact, well-muscled build, the Quarter Horse-type conformation being generally favored. Emphasis is laid on strong, correct legs and feet, because most of the breed work as stock or pleasure horses, or compete in various events, especially Western-style events.

Left **The Nez Percé tribe developed the forebears of the modern breed of Appaloosa, one of the most popular breeds in America. An Appaloosa does not necessarily have to be spotted; but, if it is not, the skin must be mottled beneath the coat hair; the hoofs must be striped, and there must be white sclera around the eyes.**

CHARACTER The Appaloosa is known for its generally calm, willing, good-natured temperament. Hence, they make ideal family ponies and horses.
PHYSIQUE Well-muscled with short back; strong legs; powerful hindquarters; hard, vertically striped hoofs; slightly sloping croup; workmanlike head with short, pointed ears; short to medium length neck; prominent withers; sloping shoulders; sparse mane and tail; alert eyes.
FEATURES Strong; hardy; versatile; good endurance.
COLOR Although there are six main coat patterns within the breed, the many variations of mottling, splashing, and spotting can sometimes make it hard to name a color or pattern with precision. The blanket pattern includes a large white area over the hindquarters.
USES Riding.
HEIGHT Mainly 14.2hh and 15.2hh.

ANCESTRY

Spotted and mottled horses were prized among ancient civilizations, although Appaloosas are not the only types with these colorings. Most types originated in Asia, spread to Europe, and were taken from there to the Americas by the conquistadors. Mainly of Oriental-type ancestry, they do however, possess some colder-type blood, probably from European ancestors, as shown by their stockier build.

Chincoteague

In 1947, author Marguerite Henry published a book entitled *Misty of Chincoteague*, which chronicles the small wild ponies that occupy Assateague Island, off the eastern coast of the United States.

The book, which continues to delight children today, drew international attention to a herd of wild ponies that are presumed to have come to the island either as strays released by early settlers on the mainland, or, according to a more romantic theory, as refugees from a Spanish ship that sank off the coast of the ponies' contemporary island home. Regardless of their origin, the ponies have long been considered unique American treasures.

Some controversy has followed the management of this unique pony through the years. Each year in July, the ponies are rounded up and swum across the water to the neighboring island of Chincoteague, where, under the guidance of the Chincoteague Volunteer Fire Department, a selected few are chosen to be adopted by members of the public. In previous years, animal welfare groups have objected to this practice, which too often resulted in the premature separation of foals from their dams, and in the negligent care of the ponies by inexperienced adopters. Cooperation between these groups and the Fire Department has now resulted, however, in improvements in the care and handling of these unique creatures. Veterinarians, animal welfare representatives, and equine educators now all work together to ensure that the ponies are delivered into proper hands.

Left The Chincoteague ponies are believed to descend from horses shipwrecked on the islands about 300 years ago.

Above Given their island existence, the Chincoteague had to survive on poor feed and rugged terrain, making them tough and hardy.

CHARACTER The Chincoteague ponies are generally very hardy. They are wise and gentle, and very receptive. Hence, it is easy to train them to suit one's requirements.
PHYSIQUE Straight head; some weakness in the legs and hindquarters.
FEATURES Hardy; personable if handled properly.
COLOR Most solid colors and pinto patterns.
USES Child's pony if properly trained; also roams wild.
HEIGHT 12hh to 13hh.

ANCESTRY
Various English and Spanish bloodlines.

Pony of the Americas

Most ponies from the United States were originally imported from other nations. However the United States does have one pony to call its own: Pony of the Americas, or POA.

This attractive animal, whose conformation is more horse-like than pony-like, sports what has long been considered a very American equine characteristic: the spotted patterns of the Appaloosa. Not surprisingly, the POA's roots are with the Appaloosa, small representatives of which were crossed in the 1950s with Arabians and various small horses of Appaloosa coloring, to create a well-built,

brightly patterned American pony. The pony has rocketed in popularity in a relatively short period of time, which is hardly surprising, considering the immense popularity of its larger spotted cousin.

Though the POA was bred originally for western events, its talents for dressage and jumping are now gaining it entrance to all manner of equine endeavor.

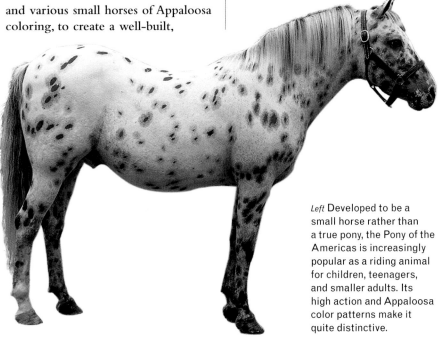

Left Developed to be a small horse rather than a true pony, the Pony of the Americas is increasingly popular as a riding animal for children, teenagers, and smaller adults. Its high action and Appaloosa color patterns make it quite distinctive.

Above **The high action and Appaloosa color patterns of the Pony of the Americas make it quite distinctive.**

CHARACTER The Pony of the Americas is specifically bred to be a small horse rather than a true pony. It is quiet and docile and an excellent all-rounder. It is tough and hardy, undemanding, and easy for children to handle.

PHYSIQUE Well-proportioned and athletic; Arab-like, wedge-shaped head with small, pricked ears; slightly dished face; broad forehead; large eyes, and a small muzzle with flaring nostrils; short back; deep chest; sloped shoulders; good muscle overall.

FEATURES Athletically versatile; interactive; great for young riders.

COLOR Appaloosa spots and characteristics like white sclera, mottled skin, some striped hoofs.

USES Riding.

HEIGHT 11.2hh to 13.2hh.

ANCESTRY

Originally bred from Shetland and Appaloosa blood. Now there is a good deal of Quarter Horse and Arab in the breed. The founding breeds, will predominate, but any pony meeting the admittedly strict registration requirements should be eligible, regardless of background.

Canadian Cutting Horse

People who do not live in North America may not realize that cattle ranching is a major business in Canada. Canada, although it has no indigenous horse breeds of its own, has long been breeding excellent horses of many types. One such type is the recognized Canadian type,

called the Canadian Cutting Horse. This horse, as its name suggests, is used in ranching, specifically for cutting cattle out from a herd. The Canadian Cutting Horse is larger than most Quarter Horses, but is just as agile, quick off the mark, and fast at the gallop over short distances.

Left This horse is yet to be recognized as a distinct breed, and is recognized only as a type.

Right This Canadian Cutting Horse clearly shows the Quarter Horse type sought in the breed, but has the typically slightly lighter frame and longer back, making it a popular choice for working with cattle.

CHARACTER Active, well-balanced, strong, and intelligent, with an instinctive cow sense. It has a tractable nature and good temperament.
PHYSIQUE Longer in the body than the Quarter Horse with a slightly convex profile.
COLOR Any.
USES Cutting contests; rodeo.
HEIGHT 15.2hh to16.1hh.

ANCESTRY

Contains much American Quarter Horse blood and is bred along the same lines and for the same qualities, but probably with a wider progenitor base of imported European stock.

Rocky Mountain Pony

Although there are only a few hundred Rocky Mountain Ponies remaining, it seems inevitable that it will, in due course, take its place among the many excellent and distinctive American breeds, and its numbers will subsequently increase.

Below This pony shows the typical coat coloring of the Rocky Mountain Pony, which, despite having only been developed for about ten years, shows much more consistent type than many older breeds.

CHARACTER The Rocky Mountain Pony is sensible, with a calm temperament. It is nimble, sure-footed, and easy to manage.

PHYSIQUE Wide chest; sloping shoulders; bold eyes; well-shaped ears; strong limbs.

FEATURES Strong; good stamina and endurance; has inherited the Iberian amble; offers a comfortable ride.

COLOR The coat is chocolate brown, often dappled, with flaxen manes and tails. Very few facial markings are acceptable, but no white is permitted above the knee or hock.

USES Riding; working with cattle.

HEIGHT 14.2hh to 14.3hh.

ANCESTRY

Like most American native breeds, the Rocky Mountain Pony also comes from old Iberian stock.

Mustang

The word Mustang comes from the Spanish *mestengo* or *mesteho*, meaning "stranger" or "outsider." Mustangs are descendants of the horses brought over by Columbus and the Spanish conquistadors.

While their story is romantic, their circumstances have not always been so. Since their arrival, Mustangs have had to wrestle with opposition. They were destroyed by ranchers and settlers who deemed them unnecessary competition for grazing lands and water earmarked for domestic livestock. But in the early 1970s, federal action was taken to end mistreatment and mass extermination of America's Mustangs, which are now protected under the law.

CHARACTER Fiercely independent and intractable.
PHYSIQUE Lightweight; sturdy build; tough legs and feet.
FEATURES Romantic past; feral; athletic.
COLOR All colors, plus pinto and Appaloosa patterns.
USES Riding when properly trained; stockwork; also run wild.
HEIGHT 14hh to 15hh.

Below The Kiger Mustang is regarded by its enthusiasts as probably being the purest breed of Mustang because it has more of the features of its Spanish ancestors than any others.

ANCESTRY
Barb ancestry is favored. Arab and Andalusian characteristics are also popular in this breed.

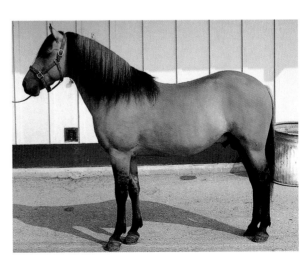

Morgan

When the small bay stallion named Figure first appeared in colonial America, it was dismissed for its small size. However, its owner (and namesake) Justin Morgan was able to rent him out to a Vermont farmer, who soon discovered that this diminutive animal was nothing short of a wonder horse.

With almost supernatural strength, speed, stamina, as well as a sweet disposition, Figure became a legend in Vermont, and was later immortalized in Marguerite Henry's book *Justin Morgan Had A Horse*.

The Morgan was also renown for being unbeatable in pulling contests and races, and went on to found the dynasty that is now known as the hardworking Morgan breed.

Left Morgan horses are all-round, family horses. They have great personality, but are tractable and willing. To this day, all of them are very much alike, having taken after their founding stallion, Figure.

Left Two types of Morgan have now developed, although they do not seem to be able to be bred with certainty. The Park Morgan has the neck set high on the shoulders, and has an upright, showy action. The Pleasure Morgan is less exaggerated in these features. The difference is mainly seen when the horses are in action.

CHARACTER Spirit, tractability, and willingness are the Morgan's hallmarks. They are hardy and quite frugal, so are reasonably easy to handle.

PHYSIQUE Wide-set pointed ears; expressive eyes and flaring nostrils; well-defined and moderately long withers, always higher than the croup; medium-size head carried high; straight or slightly concave profile; well-shaped neck, finely tapering toward the throat; elegant, yet strong and sturdy legs; rounded, hard feet; short, level, and strong back; slightly rounded and well-muscled quarters.

FEATURES Intelligent; alert; fast; versatile.

COLOR Bay, brown (often attractively dappled), black, and chestnut, with moderate white markings permitted on head and lower legs.

USES Riding; working with cattle.

HEIGHT About 14hh to 15.2hh.

ANCESTRY

This is in dispute, but it is likely to be Welsh Cob/Thoroughbred/ native American stock of Iberian/Oriental origin, plus imported European breeds.

Tennessee Walking Horse

With humble beginnings as a basic transportation horse in nineteenth century Tennessee, the Walker was bred as a sure-footed horse with enough stamina to comfortably carry a rider for hours over rough terrain.

In addition to being comfortable to ride and of sound constitution, the breed also proved to be striking in appearance. During the nineteenth century, plantation owners surveying their domain, country doctors making house calls, and traveling preachers all found their equine wishes granted with the creation of the Tennessee Walker.

Recent history has spelled controversy for this breed, now a popular show horse throughout the United States. The conflict arose several years ago over the illicit practice of soring, in which painful chemicals and equipment are applied to the horse's feet to cause it to lift them higher when performing the gait known as the running walk. This led to the passage of the American Horse Protection Act and many lawsuits.

Above Famous for its fast, running walk, this breed is extremely popular as a show, general pleasure, and harness horse.

CHARACTER Temperament is gentle and tractable, and its distinctive gaits, particularly its running walk, are desirable.

PHYSIQUE Short neck and back; strong hindquarters; sloping croup; well-boned legs; large head; pricked ears; straight profile; gentle eyes; big nostrils.

FEATURES Kind disposition; comfortable ride.

COLOR Mostly black, with chestnut, bay, brown, gray, and roan. Some white on head and lower legs is permitted.

USES Riding; family horse.

HEIGHT 15hh to 16hh.

ANCESTRY

A breed created by settlers and pioneers, the Tennessee Walking Horse is founded on Standardbred and Morgan blood with Narragansett Pacer, Saddlebred, Thoroughbred, and Canadian Pacer infusions.

Left Having an equable temperament and being easy to care for, the Tennessee Walking Horse is a rewarding, yet not too demanding, horse to own.

American Shetland

The first arrival of Shetland ponies into America took place in 1885 when Eli Elliot imported 75. The hot, humid climate in the southeastern states, where breeding was concentrated, was very different from the bitterly cold subarctic homeland conditions which had forged the ponies' small, rotund shape and short legs. However, it seems that the early imports adapted well, and there are now believed to be around 50,000 American Shetlands in the United States.

The American Shetland bears little resemblance to the true Shetland Pony because it has been created to meet local requirements, although it does retain the thick Shetland mane and tail hair. It also shows definite horse rather than pony character, and is longer in the body and leg.

Right The American Shetland has been purposely bred to be longer in the body and the leg than the true (Scottish) Shetland. It has a horse rather than pony character, and more scope than the original Shetland.

CHARACTER Tractable enough for children to handle, it is intelligent, and easy to care for.

PHYSIQUE Short neck; well-set tail with luxurious, strong hair; long but strong legs; sometimes plain and long head; straight profile with fairly long ears. Feet are often grown unnaturally long to encourage a high, flashy action but, when natural, are strong and well proportioned.

FEATURES Strong, but lacks the Shetland hardiness; more versatile than its ancestor.

COLOR All solid colors. Also roan, cream, and dun.

USES Riding; harness–racing; driving.

HEIGHT Up to 11.2hh.

ANCESTRY

Pure Shetland Ponies were crossed with Hackney Ponies, small Arabs, and Thoroughbreds to create this modern breed.

Standardbred

While England is home to the Thoroughbred, the United States boasts an illustrious racer of its own — the Standardbred.

Despite its name, breed standardization had nothing to do with the founding of the Standardbred, which was developed in the early nineteenth century to satisfy American passions for the sport of harness racing. The name refers to the practice later in the century of registering only those horses that could pace or trot a mile within a standard time.

While not a beautiful horse in the classic sense, it is considered exceptionally good-natured in temperament. After some training, Standardbreds acclimatize well to civilian life.

Left The Standardbred is the world's best harness racer. In order to produce harness racers that naturally pace or trot, precise development is required. Pacers are marginally faster than trotters, and can attain speeds today of less than 2 min for a mile (1.6 km).

Above In the United States, harness racing — both pacing and trotting — appears to be more popular than Thoroughbred racing. Such races are also popular in Canada, Scandinavia, Australia, and New Zealand. The Standardbred has been used to improve other trotting breeds throughout the world.

ANCESTRY

A mixture of breeds and types, all renowned for trotting and pacing.

CHARACTER Docile and easy to handle, willing, enthusiastic, and energetic, with a natural competitive streak.

PHYSIQUE Strong, wide loins; long, deep, and very powerful quarters with a slight slope to the tail; big, strong joints; well-defined tendons; short cannons; legs shorter than the Thoroughbred's; upper parts, particularly the thighs, are very well developed; medium to long muscular neck; very powerful, wide, deep and well-muscled shoulders; deep, well-sprung barrel; head set onto the neck at the same angle as the shoulder; tough and well-formed feet; large, mobile nostrils.

FEATURES Athletic; graceful.

COLOR Most have a brown body. Bay colors also occur where the mane and tail are black. Black, chestnut, gray, and roan colors occur more rarely.

USES Harness racing; riding; driving.

HEIGHT 14hh to 16hh.

Missouri Fox Trotter

The Missouri Fox Trotter was developed in the early nineteenth century in the Missouri and Arkansas regions by settlers who wanted a comfortable, equable natured, enduring, and speedy horse to carry them over varying terrain.

In the early days, Fox Trotters were raced, but when racing was made illegal, the Fox Trotter became a utility, all-purpose horse. A stud book was not founded until 1948.

Compared with America's other two gaited horses, the Saddlebred and the Tennessee Walking Horse, the Fox Trotter's tail is not nicked and set. It also has a lower, much less extravagant action, which cannot be altered as the breed society prohibits the use of any artificial training aids to accentuate the gait.

CHARACTER The Missouri Fox Trotter has a very tractable temperament, is sound and tough, and a willing worker.

PHYSIQUE Medium, well-formed neck, carried fairly low; moderately prominent withers; short and level back; fairly low-set tail; fine legs; large and well-formed joints; good, strong feet; well proportioned and plain head; straight profile; longish, pricked ears; generous, calm eyes; neat, squarish muzzle with open nostrils.

FEATURES Great stamina; versatile. The fox-trotting gait (in which the front feet walk actively and the hind ones trot) is the breed's distinguishing feature.

COLOR Chestnut in many variations; also brown, bay, black, gray, paint, or pinto (piebald or skewbald), and some red roans; white on head and legs.

USES Leisure riding; showing; endurance riding.

HEIGHT 14hh to 16hh.

ANCESTRY
The initial gene base was Morgan, early Thoroughbred, Arab, and old Barb-based Iberian. Later, Saddlebred and Tennessee Walking Horse blood was also used.

Left Although little known elsewhere, the equable nature of the Missouri Fox Trotter, and its hardiness and willingness to work, make it very popular in its homeland.

Palomino

The word "Palomino" has been around for a long time, having existed all over the world as a natural genetic coat-color expression in all types of horses. Having deemed the Palomino a color breed, American Palomino registries now welcome horses of all backgrounds, as long as they satisfy the color requirement of being three shades darker or lighter than the color of a newly minted gold coin.

The name "Palomino" is presumed to have come about when Queen Isabella of Spain gave some of these golden-colored horses to Cortés to take to the Americas, who on arrival presented one to Juan de Palomino.

When California came into American ownership in the mid-nineteenth century, the Palomino was rediscovered and soon became known as "The Golden Horse of the West." It came to be associated most closely with the American West, as Western show events became considered natural venues for Palomino competitors. Its popularity has not waned to this day.

Palominos have not only delighted parade, screen, and show audiences, but also inspired the formation of surprisingly enthusiastic fan clubs during the peak of their huge popularity.

CHARACTER Varies with breed, usually intelligent.
PHYSIQUE Varies with breed, but riding horse type.
FEATURES Striking appearance.
COLOR The color of the coat should be that of a
newly minted gold coin, or up to three shades darker
or lighter, with a white, cream, or silver mane and tail.
White is permitted on head and lower legs only.
USES Riding; parades.
HEIGHT Varies with breed.

ANCESTRY

*Native Spanish stock, Mustang,
and Quarter Horse.*

Top Left Since it comes in all
sizes of horse and pony, a
Palomino can usually be
found for almost anyone or
any job.

Right Surely one of the most
beautifully colored horses in
the world, the Palomino has
always been popular for
display purposes such as
parades, circuses, and
shows of various kinds.

Pinto

Originally transported to North America via the horses of the Spanish explorers, pinto patterns were considered a gift from the spirits to Native Americans, who held painted horses in the utmost esteem. Such horses, they believed, were infused with great power, which was embodied in their natural war paint. Their broken outline provided a great disguise on raids. American cowboys also coveted horses of painted patterns, perhaps secretly sharing the Native Americans' belief that the bold colors of the Pinto's coat were symptomatic of supernatural abilities.

So enamored has the United States been of Pinto horses, that the Pinto Horse Association of America (PtHA) was established in 1947 to celebrate horses and ponies of all breeds that are marked with pinto patterns. They boast registered horses and ponies throughtout the world who display one of two recognized patterns: Tobiano or Overo. Pintos are further described by color. A "piebald" is black and white, while a "skewbald" is white and any other color.

Above Dark Warrior, Grandeur Arabians, Florida, United States.

CHARACTER Depends on breed, but usually intelligent and enduring.
PHYSIQUE Depends on breed, can include Atock, Saddle, Hunter, and gaited types.
FEATURES Eye-catching; unique.
COLOR All colors (skewbald and piebald) in Tobiano and Overo patterns.
USES Depends on breed; popular in shows.
HEIGHT Depends on breed.

ANCESTRY
Various breeds of American and European origin.

Left The Pinto shown here exhibits classic Tobiano pattern, with characteristic uniformly shaped splashes of color that extend across back, flanks, and head. Pinto coloring was found in previous centuries in several breeds which now appear only in solid colors. In some countries, this horse would simply be called a skewbald.

South America

Azteca

The Azteca is one of the newest horse breeds in the world. As its name suggests, it originates from Mexico, and replaces the Mexican strain of Criollo, which is now believed to be virtually extinct.

Breeding began in 1972, when Andalusian stallions were crossed with South American Criollo and Quarter Horse mares. These breeds were carefully selected, as the aim was to create a breed with the very best qualities of the Andalusian and the Quarter Horse — both compact in build and powerfully muscled, without being heavy. The purpose of retaining some Criollo blood was to maintain a link with the traditional Mexican horse, while providing the Azteca with hardiness, toughness, soundness, and stamina, all of which abound in the Criollo.

CHARACTER The Azteca has the noble attitude and bearing of the Andalusian, with the docility of the Quarter Horse.

PHYSIQUE Elegantly arched, substantial, and well-muscled neck; fine and strong legs with good joints; muscular upper parts; good riding pasterns and feet; noble, lean head; small and pricked ears; straight or slightly convex profile with readily flared nostrils.

FEATURES Tough; fast; agile.

COLOR All colors are allowed with the exception of parti-colors.

USES Leisure riding; competition.

HEIGHT Mares average 14.3hh, while stallions average 15hh.

ANCESTRY
The Azteca is made up of a judicious blend of Andalusian, Quarter Horse, and Crillo.

Left Although a new breed, the ancient origins of the Azteca can be clearly seen in this photograph. Originally bred for leisure riding and competition work, the Azteca was meant to be non-Thoroughbred in character.

Galiceño

The Galiceño's name reflects its origins in the ponies of Galicia, northern Spain. The original ponies that traveled across the Atlantic landed in Mexico and, although used by man, bred indiscriminately among themselves. The present type therefore evolved as a result of natural selection, rather than artificial selection.

CHARACTER The Galiceño is intelligent, kind, courageous, with a lovely temperament.
PHYSIQUE Straight shoulders; narrow chest; short back; fine legs; quality head; perceptive eyes; medium-length ears; open nostrils.
FEATURES Tough; hardy; alert; fast; enduring.
COLOR Bay, black, chestnut, dun, and gray. Parti-colors and albino are not allowed.
USES Ranch work; light harness work; competition; children's pony.
HEIGHT 12hh to 13.2hh.

ANCESTRY

Descended from the Spanish pony, the Garrano is from Galicia in northwestern Spain, and also from the north Portuguese Minho.

Right Much less famous than its related Iberian breeds, the Galiceño is more Arab in type. Its fast, running, four-beat walk and good stamina carry riders comfortably and fast, over long distances.

Mangalarga

The Brazilian Mangalarga was founded in the middle of the nineteenth century by Emperor Peter II. To create the Mangalarga breed, the original, Andalusian, and other Altér Real stallions were mated with South American Criollo mares.

Like many horses of Iberian origin, the Mangalarga's gaits are not limited to walk, trot, canter, and gallop. It has a characteristic fifth gait called the *marcha* or *marchador*, which are gaucho terms. The *marcha* is a fast, rolling gait, halfway between a trot and a canter, which can be maintained for long distances.

CHARACTER The Mangalarga is sure-footed, and very cooperative.
PHYSIQUE Longish head; medium-length ears; short back; open nostrils; attractively shaped, high-held neck; long, hard legs with well-muscled upper parts; big joints; low-set tail.
COLOR Bay, gray, chestnut, and roan.
USES Stock work; riding; parades; show ring.
HEIGHT 15hh.

Below The Mangalarga's unique gait is very comfortable and fast, and can be maintained over long distances.

ANCESTRY
Altér Real, Andalusian, and Criollo blood were mixed to create this tough riding horse.

Paso Fino

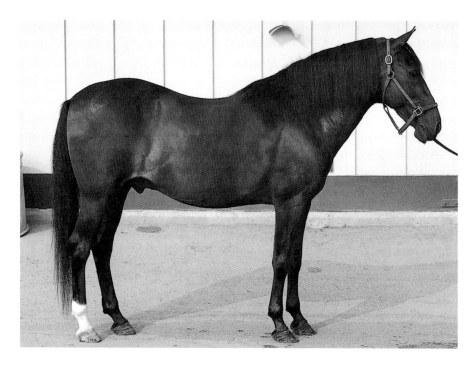

The Paso Fino is probably the most famous of the three main types of South American gaited horse. Hailing from Puerto Rico, the Paso Fino exhibited a fiery spirit called brio, a dramatic appearance, and a unique and comfortable lateral, four-beat gait called the *paso fino*. It performs the *paso corto*, the *paso fino*, and the *paso largo* with grace and skill.

Two other variants of the basic gaits at which the Paso Fino excels are the *sobre paso* and the *andadura*. In the *sobre paso*, the horse is relaxed and natural on a loose rein; this gait is not used in the show ring. In the *andadura*, the horse performs a fast lateral pacing gait, which is not comfortable, and used only for short distances when speed is of the essence.

Above The Paso Fino is best known for its showy, dishing gaits in parades, and performing the *paso corto*, the *paso fino* (or *fino fino*), and the *paso largo*.

CHARACTER The Paso Fino has an exceptionally gentle temperament, and is intelligent and easy to handle.

PHYSIQUE Arab-type head; strong back and quarters; long and pointed ears; expressive and proud eyes; hard fine legs; fine skin; silky coat hair; sensitive, open nostrils.

FEATURES Spirited; graceful; agile.

COLOR All colors.

USES Display; transportation; leisure riding; showing; parade; working horse, largely on coffee plantations.

HEIGHT Between 14.2hh and 15hh.

ANCESTRY

As with the Peruvian Stepping Horse, Barb plus old Iberian strains make up the foundation of the Paso Fino breed.

Right The ancestors of the Paso Fino, horses of Andalusian and Spanish Jennet blood, were passengers on Christopher Columbus' ship during his second voyage to the Americas. These horses were delivered to the Caribbean island now known as Dominican Republic, where they provided the foundation for the emergence of the Paso Fino.

Peruvian Stepping Horse

The Peruvian Stepping Horse, or Peruvian Paso, is the blood brother of the Paso Fino. However, each breed has subsequently evolved different characteristics in order to adapt to the climates of their respective habitats.

The Peruvian Stepping Horse was developed to carry riders comfortably for long distances over rough and treacherous mountainous terrain and narrow, rocky tracks, at high altitudes. Its exceptionally large, strong heart and lungs enable it to perform athletically, even under low oxygen levels. The horse also possesses "mountain sense," or the instinct to pick its way without fear over rocky ground, sliding shale, deep water, and steep inclines.

There are several Paso breeds which have a natural ability to perform the distinctive four-beat lateral gaits. Riders can therefore be carried at speed for long distances without tiring the horse. There are three major Paso gaits: the *paso corto*, the elegant *paso fino*, and the extended, fast *paso largo*.

Left The Peruvian Stepping Horse has evolved into a slightly different type from its brother breed, the Paso Fino. It works at high altitude, and has developed a larger, stronger heart.

Above The Peruvian Stepping Horse is independent, calm, and sure-footed.

CHARACTER The Peruvian Stepping Horse is calm, energetic, and a willing worker.
PHYSIQUE Medium-sized head; pricked, mobile ears; bright eyes; fine, strong, and well-muscled legs; flexible joints; long, sloping pasterns; open feet; very long hind legs; small muzzle with flaring nostrils.
FEATURES Tough; hardy; strong; agile.
COLOR Any color, but usually bay or chestnut. White on head and legs is permitted.
USES Riding; parade work; showing; travel and ranching.
HEIGHT 14hh to 15.1hh.

ANCESTRY

Barb plus old Iberian strains are the foundation of the Peruvian Stepping Horse, which has subsequently developed its own characteristics due to conditions in the Peruvian mountains.

Criollo

The Crillo descended from the Iberian and Oriental horses that Spanish explorers such as Cortés and Pizarro brought to America in the sixteenth century. Well suited to hostile environments, most Criollo breeds today live in a semi-wild state on the vast ranches of the southern continent. There are now several variations of the breed throughout South America, although they all have the same genetic base.

Left This Criollo shows the primitive dun coloring which often occurs in this breed, and stems most recently from its Iberian ancestors.

CHARACTER The Criollo is resistant to great discomfort, and is a fast and willing worker.
PHYSIQUE Short, broad head; close-set ears; small, tight muzzle; muscular neck; strong shoulders; broad chest; deep body on fine, strong legs; small feet.
FEATURES Tough; hardy; enduring.
COLOR Mainly primitive dun or mouse-brown, with dark points and dorsal stripes. Brown, bay, black, gray, chestnut, palomino, and roan occur, as do piebald and skewbald colors.
USES Ranch work; cattle work; endurance riding.
HEIGHT 14hh to 15hh.

ANCESTRY
This breed's ancestors were the Iberian, Barb, and Arab horses which arrived with the conquistadors.

Left Although the Crillo is known to be typically independent, it is not stubborn, and therefore makes a very good ranch horse.

Falabella

The Falabella is claimed to be the smallest horse in the world. It was created by the Falabella family on their Recrio de Roca Ranch, near Buenos Aires in Argentina. Over the years, small Thoroughbreds, Shetlands, and Arabs have been used to produce this miniature horse.

Despite its small size, the Falabella is a horse and not a pony because it has horse character and proportions.

Continual breeding for smaller size has unfortunately resulted in inherited and congenital physical weaknesses in this animal. Even the best-conformed Falabellas do not have the correct strength in relation to their size, and tend to need a lot of care and attention.

Below As a miniature horse rather than a pony, the ideal Falabella should have horse-like proportions and character.

ANCESTRY

The breed was founded by intially crossing Shetland and Thoroughbred blood, and later adding Arab blood.

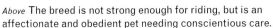

Above The breed is not strong enough for riding, but is an affectionate and obedient pet needing conscientious care.

CHARACTER The temperament of the Falabella is usually quiet, friendly, and very obedient.

PHYSIQUE Small ears set wide apart; friendly and calm eyes; straight profile; small and open nostrils; fine bones; small feet.

COLOR Appaloosa-type markings are very common, but there is a wide variety of other colors including black, bay, brown, gray, and roan.

USES Unsuitable for riding but ideal as pets, in shows, and for pulling small vehicles.

HEIGHT Not exceeding 30 inches (76 cm.).

Britain & Ireland

Dartmoor Pony
Dales Pony
Fell Pony
Shetland Pony
Welsh Cob
Welsh Mountain Pony
New Forest Pony
Thoroughbred
Clydesdale
Hackney
Cleveland Bay
Shire
Irish Draught
Exmoor Pony
Highland Pony
Anglo-Arab
Suffolk Punch
Connemara

Dartmoor Pony

The Dartmoor Pony hails from the steep, rugged moors of southwest England, a defining and ancient ancestry that has made this pony tough, sure-footed, easy to keep, and a popular choice for a variety of historical callings. First documented officially in the 1012 will of a Saxon bishop, Aelfwold of Crediton, the Dartmoor Pony was, for centuries, called to duty for everything from working in tin mines, to farming and carrying riders across rugged trail.

Demand for the pony often waned, many times to the point of extinction. However, the pony was constantly revived through infusions of blood from such breeds as Arabians and Welsh Mountain Ponies, which has resulted in the Dartmoor Pony of today, a pony renowned for its elegance and smooth gait. The Dartmoor is now considered to be both an ideal first pony for children, as well as catering to more experienced adults.

Below The Dartmoor is frequently used to produce larger saddle ponies, an endeavor that is especially successful when crossed with Arabians or Thoroughbreds.

Above The Dartmoor is an example of an indigenous breed which, although having been subject to infusions of other blood, has largely retained its original characteristics.

CHARACTER The Dartmoor has a quiet, sensible, and kind nature.

PHYSIQUE Good front; medium back; muscular hindquarters; small head with small ears; wide forehead; soft, inquisitive expression.

FEATURES Elegant; intelligent; tough; hardy; strong; smooth horse-like gait. When moving, it hardly shows any knee flexion, having a free, long, and low stride.

COLOR Brown and bay are most common. Excessive white markings on legs and head discouraged; no pinto.

USES Riding; occasionally driven.

HEIGHT Up to 12.2hh.

ANCESTRY

The Dartmoor has mixed blood for a native pony, having received infusions of Roadster, Welsh Cob, Arab, and, most recently, Thoroughbred blood.

Dales Pony

The Dales Pony is the only native British breed that has never been truly wild. It hails from the Yorkshire hills and dales on the eastern side of the Pennine hills, which run down the northern half of England.

At one time there was little distinction between the Fell Pony and the Dales Pony, and both types were informally known as Pennine ponies. However, the requirements of the regional human population eventually cultivated the stock into different types.

Right Dales Ponies are considerd best for trekking.

CHARACTER Dales Ponies have particularly hard legs and feet, and are able to withstand harsh outdoor conditions. They are quiet, but show intelligence and personality.

PHYSIQUE Strongly built; exudes strength and energy; legs sturdy with big, strong joints; a little silky feather around the fetlocks; feet hard and blueish; thick and wavy mane and tail; short ears, bright, lively eyes; mobile nostrils.

FEATURES Strong, good stamina; tough; hardy.

COLOR Usually black with some browns, bays, and grays. Little white on feet and face.

USES Light riding; trekking; driving.

HEIGHT Up to 14.2hh.

ANCESTRY

The indigenous Celtic pony was crossed with Friesian and probably French Ariègeois horses brought over to England by the Romans. In the early nineteenth century, Welsh Cob blood was introduced, as was Clydesdale blood for added size.

Fell Pony

The Fell Pony is closely related to the Dales Pony, but is smaller and of purer blood. It comes from the western side of the Pennine hills. The Fell Pony is a true mountain and moorland pony, still mostly bred and running free on the hills, although some are bred on farms and private studs.

CHARACTER The Fell Pony has an iron constitution, with typical pony character and a wild air. It has a friendly, willing, yet determined nature; and is sure-footed.

PHYSIQUE Elegant but not fine; proud outlook; showy action with a long, smooth stride; well–chiseled head; moderately wide–apart ears; broad forehead; prominent, gentle, intelligent eyes; head tapers slightly to the muzzle.

FEATURES Strong; sure-footed.

COLOR Black is the most common color, but brown, bay, and gray occur. White markings are not favored, but a small star on forehead and some white on the feet is permitted.

USES Trekking; an excellent children's pony; also good in harness.

HEIGHT Not exceeding 14hh.

ANCESTRY
The Fell Pony contains Celtic pony type plus Friesian and Galloway blood.

Right The Fell Pony is an excellent harness animal.

Shetland Pony

The Shetland Pony, the smallest of all the pony breeds, hails from the Shetland Islands off the coast of Scotland, where the terrain is rugged, the climate harsh, and the animals — ponies, cattle, and even dogs — are small in size, but tough and smart. They are presumed to be the progeny of horses brought to the islands by the Vikings, conquerors, and explorers that sporadically visited hundreds of years ago. It is now a well recognized pony, and even people who don't know horses know the Shetland Pony. The Shetland is also often the first representative of the equine species with which youngsters have contact.

Below Shetlands are active workers under saddle.

Left The Shetland Pony is a true cold-climate equine, with a rounded body, short legs, thick mane, forelock, and tail hair; wide neck, and relatively large head, which are all features that help retain heat in the body.

CHARACTER Not always trustworthy, they can be domineering, headstrong, and fiercely independent. Their occasional inclination to bite means that not all of them are entirely suitable for children.

PHYSIQUE Short, stocky, and compact; round, well-muscled hindquarters; powerful shoulders; hard feet; lush mane and tail; small ears and nostrils prevent heat loss; short, deep, and strong neck; body coat fairly fine and tough in summer, and extremely thick, long, and dense in winter, with an apparent soft under layer for extra insulation.

FEATURES Sure-footed; wise; extraordinarily strong.

COLOR Black is classic, but chestnut, bay, piebald, and skewbald are also common.

USES Riding; light driving.

HEIGHT Measured in inches (or centimeters) rather than hands. The average height is 40 inches (10 cm), but considerably smaller animals are quite usual.

ANCESTRY

In the absence of proof of any other theory, it is generally accepted that the Shetland Pony is one of the purest descendants of the primitive Celtic Pony, of which the Exmoor Pony is another example.

Welsh Cob

The Welsh Cob probably came into existence in its present-day form in the eleventh century. It was known then as the Powys Cob and also the mainly dun-colored Powys Rouncy, which was a warhorse used by a knight's squire.

Prior to that development, Welsh Mountain Ponies had been crossed with stock imported by the Romans to create a larger, stronger animal. From the eleventh to thirteenth centuries, however, Spanish/ Andalusian and Barb horses were imported. The Crusaders also brought home Arab horses, the spoils of war, which were used on the existing native stock.

As often happens when native breeds are "improved," the use of too much non-cob blood almost destroyed the Welsh Cob's unique type. Several old and valued strains became almost extinct, and in the 1930s many breeders failed to register their stock. The decline was halted when breeders began using only individuals showing the established cob type, which eliminated untypical qualities and restored the horse to its former glory.

Left Welsh Cobs are compact, well balanced, and strong. They are capable of light farm work, have speed and stamina for harness transportation, and the willingness for riding.

ANCESTRY

Based on the Welsh Mountain Pony. Over the centuries other blood has been introduced, but the Welsh Cob still retains the traditional type described by Romans and later historians.

CHARACTER The Welsh Cob is proud, gentle, and amenable. Ever versatile, it is an excellent all-round family animal, athletic and sure-footed.

PHYSIQUE Broad and generous chest; fairly pronounced withers; straight profile; flaring nostrils; open and strong jaw; large eyes with an interested expression; short, sharp, and alert ears; some silky feather permitted around the fetlocks; well-rounded and hard feet; short, strong back; long, muscular loins; long, muscular neck; well-rounded, long quarters; high-set tail carried proudly; sturdy, well-muscled legs.

FEATURES Strong; tough; hardy; enduring.

COLOR All colors but piebald and skewbald; white markings in moderation on head and lower legs.

USES Riding; driving; light draft.

HEIGHT Around 15hh.

Left Traditionally, Welsh Cobs were used around farms, and for transporting people.

Welsh Mountain Pony

The Welsh Mountain Pony is the smallest, oldest, and perhaps the best-known member of the legendary Welsh horse family. Presumed to have existed in its Welsh homeland since before the arrival of the Romans, it blossomed into a rugged, agile creature that exhibits an undeniable Arabian influence in its appearance. This influence is rooted in suspected crossings with visiting horses of Oriental breeding, evident today in the contemporary Welsh Mountain Pony's attractive head and well-proportioned physique.

This is a trustworthy, intelligent pony that is equally adept at jumping and driving, and is frequently considered an ideal choice for young equestrians. In addition to pursuing its own athletic callings, the Welsh Mountain Pony has provided the foundation for the other members of its family: Welsh Pony, Welsh Pony of cob type, and the Welsh Cob.

Above Many Welsh Mountain Ponies often look like small, stocky miniature Arabs due to the Arab blood in their ancestry, yet also display Celtic Pony characteristics.

CHARACTER The Welsh Mountain Ponies are intelligent, agile, and willing to work and please. Their action is smooth and flowing, with a good length of stride.

PHYSIQUE Face often dished; nostrils capable of widely flaring; short, well pricked, and alert ears; small, tapering, and soft muzzle; eyes set apart and down the head; neck of moderate length, quite arched, and set high on well-sloped shoulders; moderate withers; sturdy, straight legs that are well-muscled in forearm and gaskins; broad, strong joints; small, rounded, hard feet; tail set quite high on well-rounded, slightly sloping quarters; winter coat is particularly thick; good barrel, with well-sprung ribs; short strong back; great depth through the girth; strong loins.

FEATURES Versatile, gentle temperament; sure-footed; trustworthy; natural jumper.

COLOR Grays predominate, mainly due to the pervading influence on the breed of one of its patriarchs, Dyoll Starlight, but all colors other than piebald and skewbald are accepted.

USES Riding; driving; light draft.

HEIGHT Not over 12hh.

ANCESTRY

Some infusions of Thoroughbred and Arab blood during previous centuries have given the Welsh Mountain Pony the look of a stocky miniature Arab. In addition to the stock of primitive Celtic Pony, other native pony blood is also present in this breed.

New Forest Pony

One of Britain's renowned pony breeds, the New Forest Pony both originated from, and continues to occupy the approximately 65,000-acre New Forest in southern England, where herds of semi-wild ponies are known to have roamed since the eleventh century.

Centuries of cross-breeding with larger, more domestically-oriented horses, coupled with an often tough and varied career, have created an equally tough pony that, when taken from its forest home, has worked farms and mines, and carried riders along rugged, obstacle-laden roads with ease.

New Forests continue to embrace a semi-wild lifestyle, much to the delight of visitors to the region. As in days past, the wild (though privately owned) ponies roam their ancient homeland unencumbered, their notched tails indicating that their owners have paid the appropriate fees for grazing rights. Come fall, the ponies are rounded up in the annual "drift," in which they are evaluated for breeding by representatives of the New Forest Pony and Cattle Society.

Above New Forest Ponies have become a valued export from their home turf, their sound disposition and conformation attracting those seeking talented riding ponies.

CHARACTER Today's New Forest Pony is a recognizable breed of pony, noted for its nimble-footedness and intelligence. Broken-in ponies exhibit a friendly, calm temperament.

PHYSIQUE Classic pony-type conformation with strong, slender legs; hard feet; good joints; sloping shoulders; well-muscled hindquarters.

FEATURES Good jumper; smooth gaits; strong; fast.

COLOR Any color but parti-colors. Blue-eyed cream is also not recognized. White on head and legs is permitted.

USES Riding; light driving.

HEIGHT Up to 14.2hh..

ANCESTRY

Basic Celtic Pony with Oriental and British native pony infusions from the eighteenth century onward, particularly in the nineteenth century.

Left One of Britain's larger native ponies, the New Forest enjoys popularity as an ideal mount for teenagers and smaller adults, and is an excellent ride-and-drive animal. There are still feral ponies running on the scrubland of the New Forest.

Thoroughbred

The Thoroughbred is known as the aristocratic athlete of the horse world. As soon as a Thoroughbred foal can walk, it feels the urge to run. Granted freedom to roam the pasture alongside its dam, the foal's legs develop strength quickly, and the youngster will take flight with the energy inherent to all members of this fine breed.

The Thoroughbred was bred purely to race, for the enjoyment of the British royalty and aristocracy. Established through selective breeding throughout the seventeenth and eighteenth centuries, the Thoroughbred continues to dominate worldwide as a supreme racing breed.

This aristocratic breed is also highly valued for its considerable skills in the Olympic disciplines — dressage, three-day eventing, and show jumping — and international equestrian teams are frequently populated by a hefty complement of top-winning Thoroughbreds.

Above The Thoroughbred has a long and low shape. This streamlined conformation, with its long, slender but strong legs, allows it to use its head and neck for effective balance at high speeds.

Right Secretariat, a well-known American Thoroughbred stallion, has the head of a typical Thoroughbred — elegant, defined, with good skin, chiseled features, large nostrils that can flare easily to permit maximum air flow, and a somewhat superior air.

CHARACTER In temperament, the Thoroughbred is not as consistent or amenable as its ancestor, the Arab, and therefore needs sensitive, skilled handling. Type is variable, some show coldblooded features, while others show unmistakable Arab or Turk features. They are also noted for courage, and are highly strung.
PHYSIQUE Sloping shoulders; longish back; prominent withers; strong hindquarters; long legs; small hoofs; long neck; refined head; typically straight profile; large nostrils.
FEATURES Elegant; athletic; hotblooded.
COLOR Solid colors; brown, hay, chestnut, gray, and sometimes black; white markings on legs and head, but not on the body.
USES Racing; hunting; equestrian sports.
HEIGHT Mostly between 15.2hh and 16.2hh.

ANCESTRY
The Thoroughbred is relatively new as an official breed. The breed consists of imported Oriental stock which was mated with stock present in Britain at that time. There are many gaps in early pedigrees but it is almost certain that "racers" were bred from both indigenous and native British breeds, and other imported ones.

Clydesdale

The Clydesdale is something of a paradox. It undoubtedly belongs to the category of heavy draft horses, and is extremely well-suited to this job because of its strength and size, yet in appearance it is elegant and refined for a heavy breed. The breed originated in the Clyde Valley.

ANCESTRY

The exact ancestry of the Clydesdale is impossible to trace. However, it is almost certain that Scottish Galloway mares were mated to Flemish stallions. Friesian, Shire, and Cleveland Bay blood definitely flows in the veins of the Clydesdale.

Left Clydesdales are popular as working horses in breweries.

CHARACTER Clydesdales are strong, hardy horses with a friendly, calm, and sociable temperament. They are not sluggish despite their size, and have active, energetic gaits.

PHYSIQUE Well-muscled, wide, long, and strong quarters; short and slightly hollow back with broad, short loins; well-sloped, muscular shoulders; hind legs close but straight down; feet open and large, showing no tendency toward contraction at the heels; fairly long and arched neck; nostrils larger and more open than most heavy breeds.

FEATURES Flashy; graceful.

COLOR Commonly roan, occasionally bay, brown, black, and chestnut.

USES Heavy draft.

HEIGHT Average 16.2hh, in males often 17hh, or more.

Above The long-legged Clydesdale is one of the taller heavy breeds.

Hackney

The Hackney was the result of blending Norfolk Trotters and Yorkshire coach horses. The newly established, high-stepping breed was first enlisted as a horse for hire, and performed the function of a nineteenth-century taxicab.

Below The Hackney Horse and the Hackney Pony are show horses par excellence. A very specialized breed, they need skilled handling to control their extravagant trotting action and spirited temperament.

CHARACTER Spirited and energetic horses, not suited to novice handlers. They require expert handling.
PHYSIQUE Elegantly muscled; long neck; small head; broad chest; sloping shoulders; straight back; high-set tail; excellent feet and legs.
FEATURES Flashy; spirited; excellent show animal. The most distinguishing feature is the extravagant, ground-covering trot.
COLOR Mostly bay, brown, and black, with some chestnuts and a few rare roans. White markings are evident on head and legs.
USES Light driving; show.
HEIGHT Horse: 14hh to 15.3hh; Pony: 14hh.

ANCESTRY

The Hackney Horse includes trotting blood of various strains, with Oriental and Thoroughbred additions for quality and spirit.

Cleveland Bay

The Cleveland Bay horse has often been regarded as the typical eighteenth century carriage horse, and was often depicted pulling black carriages along cobblestone streets in England.

Long renowned for its unmatched skill as a plow, carriage, coach, pack, and all-around driving horse, the Cleveland Bay is celebrated as England's oldest established breed.

Below Until 1884, the Cleveland Bay was called The Chapman after an early traveling salesmen by the same name.

CHARACTER Ideal for all kinds of work, especially transportation. Calm and willing, it has also proved to be a reliable riding horse.
PHYSIQUE Well-muscled; deep, wide girth; medium back; deep, sloping shoulders; strong loins; level hindquarters; good joints; excellent feet; slender neck.
FEATURES Powerful; elegant; level-headed.
COLOR Bay; a small white star; some gray in the black mane and tail is permissible.
USES Riding; driving; light draft.
HEIGHT 16hh to 16.2hh.

ANCESTRY
Native Chapman Horse with later infusions of the Thoroughbred.

Shire

The Shire Horse is often depicted as a large, wise, plodding horse pulling a plow, or set in a scene by a medieval castle, with a knight in shining armour upon its back. Nothing could be further from the truth.

The Shire Horse only evolved in England during the nineteenth century, when breeding of heavy horses for agriculture and heavy haulage was concentrated in the Midlands. Previously, the heavy fenland soils and Midland clays had been very tiring for horses to work, and it was felt that a big, strong horse was needed to cope with those conditions. The breeders ultimately produced the biggest and strongest breed of horse in the world — the average Shire stood over 18 hands high and weighed just over a ton.

The Shire is a coldblooded animal, not particularly sensitive to the weather, but like all horses and ponies, appreciates shelter from extreme climates. They eat vast quantities of feeding straws, hay, some grain concentrates, and root vegetables of various kinds. Brewery horses often also eat used hops and yeast, and are even reputed to enjoy a daily allowance of about a bucket of beer.

Above The stunning black Shire often inspires an admiring crowd at England's annual Shire Horse Show.

CHARACTER The Shire is docile, gentle, hard-working, and good-tempered.

PHYSIQUE Deep and well-rounded barrel; long, arched, and strong neck; long, sloping, muscular shoulders; broad and deep chest; long, muscular, and rounded loins and hindquarters.

COLOR Black, bay or gray, with white markings.

USES Farm, show, draft, also used by the breweries to transport drays of barrels to the ale houses and inns.

HEIGHT Ranging from 17hh to 18hh and above, the Shire is the tallest horse in the world.

ANCESTRY

The Shire Horse traces its ancestors back several centuries to breeds such as the Old English Black Carthorse, Flemish, Friesian, and Native heavy stock.

Above Known as "gentle giants," Shires were developed in England in the nineteenth century to meet demands for a stronger animal capable of pulling the heavier farm machinery and transportation vehicles that were coming into use.

Irish Draught

The history of Ireland has long been entwined with that of the Irish Draught. Renowned for its rich equine culture, Ireland has long cultivated its horses to meet the unique needs of the island nation, the result being an equine population of international reputation and popularity.

Thousands of years in the making, the Irish Draught carries the blood of the small horses of the Celts, the fine horses of Spain (particularly the Andalusian), the heavy Great Horses of knights in armor, and, in later years, the Thoroughbreds of England. With access to such diverse bloodlines, Irish farmers blended an all-purpose draft horse that could not only work the fields, but also pull a cart, carry a rider on its back, and even over jumps if need be. The Irish Draught provided the foundation for the celebrated Irish Hunter.

Right The Irish Draught is a medium-heavy breed developed as an all-round working horse in Ireland. It was also used extensively by the military as a pack horse.

Below The Irish Draught, and its crosses — particularly with the Thoroughbred — has traditionally produced superb show jumpers and eventers.

CHARACTER Unexpectedly agile and enthusiastic for its type and weight, the Irish Draught is spirited, amenable, active, and courageous.

PHYSIQUE Muscular loins; sloped but strong, deep quarters; low-set tail; deep barrel; straight back; moderately prominent withers; shoulders slope above a broad, deep chest; short to medium neck; sharp ears; clean-legged, having no significant amounts of long hair around the fetlocks and heels; well-muscled legs and well-rounded hoofs.

FEATURES Versatile; proud; good jumper; athletic; good stamina; exceptional metabolism.

COLOR All solid colors, but black is rare. No parti-colors and little white on face or legs. Clean-legged with only a very slight silky feather allowed on the fetlocks. The coat is surprisingly fine considering the horse's type.

USES Riding; draft work.

HEIGHT Normally between 15hh and 17hh.

ANCESTRY

The Irish Draught is a rich mixture of primitive Celtic Pony stock, various European infusions, and Spanish and Oriental blood, including considerable Thoroughbred strains.

Exmoor Pony

The Exmoor Pony is one of the most individual, ancient, and pure pony breeds. Its origins were traced from a prehistoric, pre-Ice Age pony whose bones and fossils were found in Alaska. This cold climate, coupled with danger from many predators, forged a tough, wild pony. As the Ice Age ended, the pony migrated across the Bering land bridge to Siberia, through the Urals, and westward through Europe. The pony then crossed the land mass which has now become the English Channel, into southern England. Some wild herds still roam Exmoor.

CHARACTER Provided they are caught and broken in when young, Exmoor Ponies are willing and hard-working.

PHYSIQUE Full and wiry manes and tails; slender but strong legs; well-formed joints; small but very hard and rounded feet; fairly large head; thick, short ears; wide forehead; protruding lids to protect eyes from rain.

FEATURES Sturdy; thickset; great stamina; tough; hardy.

COLOR Bay, brown, or dun with "mealy" (oatmeal-shaded) coloring around the eyes, muzzle, inside the flanks, and sometimes under the belly. No white anywhere. Black mane, forelock, and tail.

USES Riding; trekking; endurance riding.

HEIGHT Up to 12.3hh for stallions, up to 12.2hh for mares.

ANCESTRY
A primitive type with hardly any other blood.

Below The Exmoor Ponies still run wild on Exmoor, yet make excellent family ponies if caught young.

Highland Pony

Apart from in the Highlands themselves, types of Highland Pony are also present on the islands of Skye, Jura, Uist, Barra, Harris, Tiree, Lewis, Arran, Rhum, Islay, and Mull.

Traditionally, there were two main types of Highland Pony, a small island type and a larger, heavier mainland type known as a "Garron." Today, the Highland Pony Society recognizes only one pony, as interbreeding has largely done away with the two main types, although both small and larger Highlands can now be found.

CHARACTER Highland Ponies are known for their extremely kind and cooperative temperament, yet have a spirited personality.

PHYSIQUE Strongly muscled legs; tough, well-shaped feet; short but broad head; short ears; bright eyes; straight profile; open and mobile nostrils; neat muzzle.

FEATURES Sturdy; great strength; zebra marks on the insides of the legs.

COLOR A wide range of shades mostly within the dun color, with names such as cream, fox, gold, yellow, and gray. Conventional grays, blacks, browns, bays, and chestnuts are also found.

USES Riding; trekking; harness.

HEIGHT From small, almost Shetland sizes (now rare) to ponies not exceeding 14.2hh.

ANCESTRY

Based on a Celtic Pony type, the now extinct Galloway was bred extensively with many Highlands. There have also been Percheron, Clydesdale, Spanish, Barb, and Arab infusions. Despite these influences, the Highland is its own recognizable type.

Right **One of Britain's large native ponies, the sturdy Highland is still used as an all-rounder, from croft working to trekking.**

Anglo-Arab

The Anglo-Arab is a combination of two of the most aristocratic breeds in the world — the Arab and the Thoroughbred. The term "Anglo" comes from the fact that the Thoroughbred is an English breed.

In Britain, the Anglo-Arab must be the product of only Arab and Thoroughbred parents. However, other countries have introduced native blood into their Anglo-Arabs. The French Anglo-Arab is an excellent example.

As the Anglo-Arab is a combination of two separate but established and prominent breeds, it is not usually regarded as an actual breed itself — one exception being the previously mentioned French Anglo-Arab.

Other variations of the Anglo-Arab breed include the Gidran (Hungarian Anglo-Arab), Shagya Arab of Hungary, the Russian Strelets Arab, and the Hispano-Arab of Spain.

Left The Anglo-Arab is a top-quality riding horse with all the hallmarks of a hotblood. A combination of the Arab and the Thoroughbred, the Anglo-Arab can take after either breed.

CHARACTER A spirited, intelligent, courageous, and affectionate nature is characteristic of the best Anglo-Arabs. They have plenty of personality and tend to be pensive, unlike some Thoroughbreds. They should be cared for with sensitivity and skill, plus plenty of exercise.

PHYSIQUE Should show unmistakable Arab ancestry, but often not as marked as the pure Arab; straight, or dished (concave) profile; moderately long, fine and pointed ears; short and fine coat, which becomes slightly longer and denser in winter; fine and silky mane and tail hair.

FEATURES Athletic; strong; good stamina.

COLOR Any of the parent colors — black (uncommon), brown, bay, chestnut, or gray. White markings on legs and head, but not on the body.

USES Riding; show jumping; endurance riding; hunting; racing.

HEIGHT Wide range, from about 14.2hh to 16.1hh, with some animals outside this range.

ANCESTRY

The true Anglo-Arab will have ancestors of only Thoroughbred and Arab blood, yet some countries have introduced the blood of their respective native horse or pony breeds.

Above Anglo-Arabs excel in most spheres of competition. In action, they should have a free-ranging stride like the Thoroughbred with the spring and comfort of the Arab.

Suffolk Punch

The Suffolk Punch, or Suffolk Horse, holds the distinction of being England's oldest pure draft breed. Though heavy horses have occupied England for thousands of years, the Suffolk, aided by the isolation of its East Anglian homeland, has existed since the sixteenth century.

Like all the heavy draft breeds, the Suffolk suffered the effects of twentieth century mechanization with varying success. While its numbers declined dramatically in the United States, the breed has maintained a healthy position in its homeland and is now a popular export.

Below The Suffolk Punch combines strength of character with generosity of spirit.

CHARACTER Suffolk Punches are well-balanced and extremely powerful smaller-sized heavy horses. They are able to thrive on moderate rations, begin work at two years of age, and work well into their twenties. They are kind natured and are willing workers.
PHYSIQUE Massive physique; short legs; deep chest and girth; crested neck; powerfully muscled hindquarters: handsome head with broad forehead.
FEATURES Docile temperament; great strength and stamina; easy to keep.
COLOR Any color but parti-colors. Blue-eyed cream is also not allowed. White on head and legs permitted.
USES Heavy draft; crossbreeding.
HEIGHT Averaging 15.3hh to 16. 1hh.

ANCESTRY

Almost certainly descended from the heavy cob-type horses of Suffolk of the tenth and eleventh centuries. The Suffolk Punch has also received infusions of trotting blood, almost certainly crosses of the imported Flanders heavy horses and, later, Thoroughbred blood.

Connemara

An ancient breed of mysterious origin, the Connemara began as a native Irish breed that was subsequently influenced by the arrival of visitors and conquerors. Through the ages the Connemara's own inherent gifts have been enhanced by infusions of a variety of bloodlines.

Although the Connemara breed is only fairly recent in origin, it is already considered one of the most refined ponies of the British Isles.

Below The name Connemara indicated the district from which the pony originated.

CHARACTER The Connemara is not susceptible to adverse weather conditions. It is sure-footed, and a willing worker. An ideal family pony, it is also docile, patient, and easy to handle.

PHYSIQUE Athletic full neck; straight back; thick mane and tail; attractive head; straight profile; deep chest; clean, well-muscled legs.

FEATURES Elegant; great stamina; good jumper.

COLOR Mainly gray; all solid colors including dun.

USES Riding; light draft.

HEIGHT From 13hh to 14.2hh.

ANCESTRY

The Connemara stems from the ancient Celtic Pony, but in recent times, has had blood introduced from various other breeds, nevertheless, it has achieved a recognizable character and retained its hardiness.

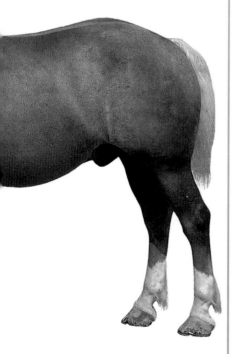

Western Europe

Selle Francais
French Trotter
Haflinger
Noriker
Lippizaner
Hanoverian
Holsteiner
Percheron
Oldenburg
East Friesian
Trakehner
Dutch Warmblood
Dutch Draft
Gelderland
Friesian
Schleswig Heavy Draft
Westphalian
Swiss Warmblood
Brabant
Breton
Norman Cob
Ardennais
Camargue

Selle Francais

French breeders have long understood the effectiveness of hybrid vigor, enlisting some of the world's finest horses, particularly those of Spanish and English extraction, to breed to their coldblooded native stock. The result of one such Norman hybrid breeding program was the distinctive Anglo-Norman, so-called because of its rich genetic mix.

The Anglo-Norman originally developed in the nineteenth century, and in the mid-twentieth century became known as the Selle Francais.

Although the Selle Francais originally shared a common background with the French Trotter, the Trotter has become one of the strongest and fastest harness racers in the world, while the Selle Francais has become what some have described as the world's greatest show jumper.

Left **A** high-quality riding and performance horse, the Selle Français exhibits considerable variety of type within its breed. The horse pictured here resembles a middleweight Thoroughbred of good conformation.

Left Miss Fan, ridden by Eddie Macken, here representing Ireland at Aachen in 1955, is a good example of a Selle Francais used for its original show jumping purpose.

ANCESTRY

The pervading influences today are Norman and Thoroughbred, plus Oriental strains and native French regional breeds. However, a strong Norfolk Roadster and Trotter influence remain.

CHARACTER Variable character is the dominant feature of the breed. In the main, the horses are docile but energetic, willing workers that are not hard to handle.

PHYSIQUE Long neck; large head; deep girth; short back; good joints, powerful hindquarters and shoulders; big boned.

FEATURES Courageous; hardy; excellent jumper.

COLOR Chestnut and bay are most common.

USES Serious riding.

HEIGHT Overall, taking into account the different types, the height varies from 15.1hh to over 16hh.

French Trotter

Native to one of Europe's premier horse-breeding regions, within decades of its founding, what is now known as the French Trotter had become a fixture as a harness racer throughtout France. The breed's skill and speed are a result of combining the Thoroughbreds and Norfolk Trotters from England, and Standardbreds from the United States.

Though it had raced throughout the nineteenth century, the French Trotter was not officially granted its own stud book until 1922.

The French Trotter is larger and more powerful than its typical counterparts, and therefore occupies a unique position in the international harness racing community. This is largely because French harness racing involves both the traditional wheeled version as well as an under-saddle variation, the latter requiring rather more strength and endurance than might be needed of a horse participating solely in the traditional style of harness racing.

Left Trotting races are particularly popular in France, both in harness and under saddle racing.

Above This animal's long back is suggestive of its French Norman ancestry.

CHARACTER The temperament, spirit, and energy of the French Trotter is similar to that of the Thoroughbred.

PHYSIQUE Strong overall, with prominent withers; sloped shoulders; powerful hindquarters; sloping croup; hard feet; straight profile.

FEATURES Races both in harness and under saddle; powerful; spirited.

COLOR Chestnut, bay, and brown are the most common, with some roans, blacks, and the rare gray.

USES Harness racing; riding.

HEIGHT Averaging around 16.2hh.

ANCESTRY

Based on the Norman and the Thoroughbred, the French Trotter also contains Norfolk Roadster, English halfbred, Hackney, Orlov Trotter, and later infusions of Thoroughbred stock with American Standardbred blood.

Haflinger

The origins of the Haflinger pony are rather obscure. What is known about the Haflinger is that all modern varieties descend from an Arab stallion, El Bedavi XXII.

Below Founded hundreds of years ago as a small, sturdy, working horse, the modern Haflinger has survived border changes in its home region between Austria and Italy. It remains an extremely popular large working pony, and is especially useful as a family pony.

CHARACTER Haflingers are docile yet bright, friendly, and trusting toward humans.

PHYSIQUE Chunky and compact in appearance; elegant, wedged shaped head; short, pointed ears; expressive, deep eyes; straight or concave profile; neat muzzle with fine, mobile nostrils.

FEATURES Strong; good stamina; enduring; sure-footed.

COLOR All shades of chestnut with striking flaxen mane, forelock, and tail. White markings are common on the head, but extremely rare on the legs.

USES Riding; children's pony; farm work; forestry.

HEIGHT Up to 14hh.

ANCESTRY
Believed to have originated from local heavy-type ponies with subsequent Oriental input.

Noriker

The Noriker (also known as Pinzgauer, Oberlander, or South German Coldblood) is an ancient breed founded from various heavy horses introduced into its homeland some 2,000 years ago by the Romans. It's name, Noricum, is derived from the name of the province the horse originated from, which was made up of roughly the area occupied by today's Styria and Carinthia in Austria.

There are five recognizable strains of Noriker today, but all can be described as being small carthorses, able to work the mountainous terrain of southern Europe.

Below The Noriker is a medium-sized heavy-type, ideal for work in mountain country.

CHARACTER The Noriker is a calm and quiet carthorse.
PHYSIQUE Short and thick neck; well muscled, strong shoulder; low-set tail; mane and tail thick and often wavy; sturdy legs with moderate feathering; slightly heavy head; convex profile; short ears; open nostrils.
FEATURES Strong; active; hardy; sure-footed.
COLOR Bay, chestnut (often with flaxen mane and tail), roan, brown, black, or spotted. Rarely gray or dappled gray.
USES Farm work; forestry.
HEIGHT From 15.1hh to 16.2hh.

ANCESTRY
An ancient breed founded on Roman imports bred with local stock. Some Andalusian and Neapolitan blood runs in its veins with, in the South German strain, added infusions of Norman, Cleveland Bay, Holstein, Hungarian, Clydesdale, and Oldenburg blood.

Lipizzaner

That General George S. Patton was fond of horses is no secret. That he possibly saved Austria's illustrious Spanish Riding School and its legendary white Lipizzaner horses from destruction may not be so widely known.

Prior to losing World War II, Hitler had chosen to spare Germany's Riding School. Before the war came to an end, the Riding School had been scattered and moved out of its Viennese home, and the school's director feared for the fate of his horses. In a dramatic move, the director presented the school and its horses to General Patton and asked that they be placed under American protection until the war's end. General Patton complied, and thus secured a safe future for the Lipizzaner.

The Lipizzaners of the Spanish Riding School are now bred at the stud in Piber. Lipizzaners also reside outside of Austria, and continue to enjoy a dedicated following of civilian horse owners.

Left The Lipizzaner shows its Iberian ancestry in its overall curvaceous, pleasing outline. This horse is somewhat lighter in type.

Left The Lipizzaner is probably most famous today for its performances at the Spanish Riding School in Vienna where the "dancing white stallions" perform *Haute École* classical airs or movements. The air shown here is the pesade.

CHARACTER A gentle but proud temperament is the hallmark of the Lipizzaner. The horse is willing, intelligent, and possesses natural balance.
PHYSIQUE Muscular overall; long head of straight or convex profile; arched neck; sloping shoulders and croup; long back; deep chest; clean joints; good feet and legs.
FEATURES Strong; good stamina; agile; natural show horse.
COLOR Born dark, lighten to gray or white with maturity.
USES Riding; light driving.
HEIGHT About 15hh to 16.1hh, although taller animals can be found.

ANCESTRY

The Lipizzaner breed is comprised of a blend of breeds containing large amounts of old Spanish blood. Today, both the riding and the larger, freer-moving carriage horses are bred from different types within the breed.

Hanoverian

Throughout its history, Hanoverian breeders have proven themselves skilled at making the necessary adjustments to their breed to meet the public's demands. In addition to its influence in the development of breeds such as the Oldenburg, Westphalian, Danish, and Dutch Warmbloods, the Hanoverian has been nimble at changing with the times, and has been refined from the large heavy draft and coach horse to a cavalry mount.

With the emergence of sport horse disciplines, the Hanoverian has also proved itseld to be a World Class competitor. Modern national equestrian teams are rich with Hanoverian representatives, who turn-over many medals in a variety of disciplines, from dressage to showjumping, to three-day eventing.

Left The Hanoverian is noted for its long action and generally excellent conformation, and excels as a dressage, show jumping, and riding horse.

Above Pictured here is Weyden, a Hanoverian ridden by Sven Rothenberger at the 1996 Olympics in Atlanta. This breed is a frequent participant in the Olympic disciplines.

CHARACTER The typical Hanoverian is of an equable temperament. It exudes self-confidence and natural pride, yet at the same time is not difficult to handle.
PHYSIQUE Big-boned, yet refined; large, sloping shoulders; muscular hindquarters; flattish croup; powerful hock action; definite Thoroughbred influence.
FEATURES Strong; athletically versatile; free and supple action.
COLOR Primarily chestnut, bay, brown, black, and gray. Often with substantial white on lower legs, and sometimes on the face.
USES Serious riding.
HEIGHT Usually between 15.2hh and 17hh.

ANCESTRY

The Hanoverian is made up of a careful blend of many horse breeds, which were substituted as required down the ages.

Holsteiner

During the fourteenth century, a monastery in the marshy area of the Elmshorn district of Schleswig-Holstein, in what is now a German state, began breeding horses. The monastery established their stud with horses of Neapolitan, Oriental, and Andalusian extraction, as well as native stock that roamed the rugged, marshy region. Soon the monks were producing premier farm and war horses that would eventually be named the Holsteiner, the oldest of Germany's warmblood breeds.

In addition to its role as a plow horse the Holsteiner was also recruited early on because of its regal appearance and action, for what would be a long and illustrious military career.

Following World War II the Holsteiner emerged as a contender on the international show scene. With Thoroughbred influence to add refinement, this calm, affectionate, rather distinct warmblood has made a name for itself as a horse that excels in jumping, dressage and eventing.

CHARACTER The Holsteiner has an excellent temperament and is of a different makeup to other warmbloods. It is a large, yet elegant, and fine performance horse.

PHYSIQUE Solid and somewhat heavy with muscular neck; prominent withers; sloping shoulders; powerful hindquarters; short back; strong legs.

FEATURES Friendly; good stamina; tough; hardy.

COLOR Most are bay, chestnut or gray.

USES Serious riding; driving.

HEIGHT Between 16hh and 17hh.

Left Apart from the overall impression of a quality, tough, large sized horse, the main feature of the Holsteiner is its strong, well-balanced, long stride.

ANCESTRY

The Holsteiner's ancestor is the Marsh Horse, with added Andalusian, Neapolitan, and Oriental infusions of blood.

Left The Holsteiner depicted here is a good example of the tall, light, quality, Thoroughbred-influenced horse most sought after by riders today.

Percheron

The Percheron is another illustrious breed to emerge from the rich horse-producing region of Normandy, France. This particular member of the Normandy family has become one of the world's most recognized draft breeds.

The ancestry of the Percheron is unclear, as its home territory was a traditional stopping place for many different cultures and thus many different horses through the centuries. What is most evident in the contemporary Percheron, however, is the heavy Arabian influence.

Today the Percheron can be seen all over the world, from Europe to Disneyland, where it is the breed of choice for the horse-drawn vehicles.

Left The Percheron is sometimes used as a heavy riding horse because it's stride and riding-horse action are unique among heavily muscled horses.

Above Percherons are still used as working horses in agriculture and haulage in France and other countries.

ANCESTRY

Mares native to the La Perche district of Normandy formed the root stock. Other European heavy breeds, plus infusions of English Thoroughbred blood, combined to produce an excellent heavy horse.

CHARACTER The Percheron is noted for its equable temperament, its intelligence, ease of handling, and willingness to work.

PHYSIQUE Heavily muscled; handsome head; prominent withers: deep chest; broad overall structure; short legs; short back; full tail and mane; heavy Arabian influence.

FEATURES Elegant; agile; strong; energetic.

COLOR Gray or black.

USES Heavy draft.

HEIGHT There is a smaller recognized variety which stands between 14.3hh and 16.1hh and a larger one, which stands between 16.1hh and 17.3hh and taller.

Oldenburg

World War II marked a turning point for the European horse community, particularly for the notoriously rich horse-breeding regions of Germany.

The Oldenburg from the Oldenburg region of northwest Germany had been hit particularly hard by progress and war, and was in danger of extinction. However, breeders lightened their horse to cater to increasing leisure pursuits of riding, and the breed eventually developed to take its place in the growing field of competitive riding.

Below The Oldenburg is an excellent carriage horse, and more increasingly, is seen in show jumping and dressage.

CHARACTER The Oldenburg is not quite as hardy or enduring as most other warmbloods, but its strength, early maturity and longevity, height, and long, active stride mean that it remains in demand.

PHYSIQUE Strong shoulders and hindquarters; deep girth; strong back; good legs and bone.

FEATURES Handsome; level-headed; good jumper.

COLOR Mainly black, brown, and bay.

USES Serious riding.

HEIGHT From about 16.2hh to 17.2hh.

ANCESTRY

The Oldenburg is based on the old Friesian type, with subsequent additions of many other breeds to give it height and strength.

East Friesian

The East Friesian is a blood brother of the Oldenburg, and both were regarded as one breed for about 300 years, until World War II split Germany in two. The East Friesian stems from the stock left in eastern Germany.

Historically, Eastern European horse breeders have been known to favor a lighter and more Oriental horse. Therefore, when the East Friesian stock was being further refined, its breeders turned to the Arab to add quality, spirit, and a lighter frame to the existing breed.

The East Friesian is a good example of how a breed can be changed until it bears virtually no resemblance to its original stock.

CHARACTER The East Friesian is an all-round, spirited, courageous, and good-natured horse.
PHYSIQUE A well-balanced, quality horse; elegant head; moderately long, pointed ears; broad forehead; large eyes set apart; straight profile; open and flaring nostrils.
FEATURES Energetic; strong; excellent stamina.
COLOR Bay, brown, black, chestnut, or gray. White is permitted on head and legs.
USES Riding; competition; harness.
HEIGHT From 15.2hh to 16.1hh.

Below Today's East Friesian bears little resemblance to its original "brother" breed, the Oldenburg.

ANCESTRY
A mix of European breeds; however, the East Friesian has more Arab and Hanoverian blood than its close relative, the Oldenburg.

Trakehner

Hailing from the celebrated Trakehnen stud in East Prussia in a region that is now part of Lithuania, the Trakehner horse has been forced to evacuate its home many times since its discovery in 1732 by Frederick William I of Prussia. Permanent evacuation occurred at the end of World War II in an epic drama that has been called the "Trek." With the Russians threatening to invade, the horses were loaded with packs and harnessed to carts for a traumatic evacuation of 500 to 900 miles to the Allied forces in what was then West Germany. Fewer than 1,000 of the 50,000 Trakehners that embarked, survived the journey.

Those Trakehners that survived were highly praised for their endurance. Though the equine refugees were at first scattered throughout Germany, in 1947 they were reunited, and the Trakehner Verband was officially established to rebuild the breed.

The combination of a tumultuous history, and a dedicated army of breeders, has resulted in a twentieth century horse that has made a name for itself in eventing and dressage.

Today, its numbers healthy, its sport-horse track record building momentum, the most elegant and versatile of all the warmbloods may now enjoy a more peaceful existence.

Left The Trakehner was developed as a high-class competition horse. This is Perow (ridden by M. Gibson) competing for the United States in the 1996 Olympic dressage competition.

Above The Trakehner is best suited for eventing, largely due to the influence of Thoroughbred blood with some heavy or pony blood. This combination provides speed, agility, and jumping ability.

CHARACTER Trakehners are courageous, versatile, spirited, yet calm and affectionate towards people.
PHYSIQUE Lighter than other warmbloods; sloped shoulders; defined withers; good joints and feet; strong back and hindquarters.
FEATURES Elegant; alert; strong; good stamina.
COLOR Most common are bay, chestnut, black, brown, and some gray.
USES Serious riding.
HEIGHT About 16hh to 16.2hh.

ANCESTRY

Based on indigenous feral blood, mixed blood was introduced in the Middle Ages and again in the eighteenth century. Subsequently, the old East Prussian type was re-selected and infused with English Thoroughbred and Arab blood.

Dutch Warmblood

While Germany is a nation already renowned for its contributions to European warmbloods, Dutch breeds such as the Dutch Warmblood are also creating an impact on sporting horse breeds.

The Dutch Warmblood is bred within a personalized, non-governmental program. The program is based on the small breeding operations of Dutch farmers, who as a community have for decades worked to sculpt this horse first into a valued farm and carriage horse with roots deep within Holland's rich agricultural traditions, and then, with the twentieth century's emphasis on equine competition, into a top-flight athlete.

Each mare and stallion used for breeding is judged and graded by officials from the breed registry, who try to put as much emphasis on temperament as they do on physical structure.

Left The Dutch Warmblood has less heavy blood in its veins than some other warmbloods. The Thoroughbred and lighter types of warmblood are also evident in this attractive horse. The Dutch Warmblood's action is particularly notable, being long, free, and possessing the elasticity demanded of today's performance horses, particularly in dressage.

Above The Dutch Warmblood was developed mainly as a show jumper and dressage horse.

CHARACTER Most Dutch Warmbloods have an excellent temperament; are normally quiet, willing, intelligent, with enough spirit and energy to command attention and perform the work required of them.

PHYSIQUE Varies with type, but a big boned athletic horse with refined features: well-muscled legs; well-ribbed body, excellent feet.

FEATURES Strong; athletically versatile; fluid action.

COLOR Typically chestnut, bay, black, and gray.

USES Riding; driving.

HEIGHT 16hh or above.

ANCESTRY

The Dutch Warmblood is mainly made up of the two Dutch native breeds, the Groningen and the Gelderlander. Thoroughbred and other warmblood types have been used to refine the breed to adjust temperament and conformation.

Dutch Draft

The modern Dutch Draft was officially registered in the early twentieth century. Great attention has since been paid to the purity of the breed, and from 1925 no horse other than those from registered parents are admitted to the stud book.

Below The Dutch Draft is certainly one of the heaviest breeds, for its height, in the world. For massive strength and moving heavy loads, it is an excellent choice, and is still a popular workhorse.

CHARACTER The Dutch Draft is a docile, willing horse. It is particularly known for its excellent fertility and intelligence.

PHYSIQUE Truly heavy and massive; strong and muscular pillar-like legs; feathering around the feet and up the backs of the legs; squarish head; prominent, massive jaws; flat forehead; short, straight ears; small eyes; narrow but mobile nostrils, capable of flaring.

FEATURES Strong; tough; active.

COLOR Chestnut, bay, or gray, occasionally black.

USES Farm work; heavy draft work.

HEIGHT The upper limit is about 17hh.

ANCESTRY

Regional heavy horses from the Low Countries almost certainly form the progenitor base with nineteenth century crosses of Brabant and Ardennais.

Gelderland

During the nineteenth century, perceiving a gap in the market for a quality carriage and riding horse, the farmers of the Dutch province of Gelder crossed native heavy mares with quality stallions imported from various European countries. The experiment resulted in the Gelderland, an all-round draft horse, which later developed into a first-class carriage horse.

CHARACTER An active, quiet, elegant carriage and saddle horse, with a mild temperament.
PHYSIQUE Elegant, compact body; strong arched neck, well-proportioned head; fine, moderately long ears; large nostrils.
FEATURES Strong; good carriage horse.
COLOR Many Gelderlands are chestnut, but bay, black, and gray are also found. There are often fairly extensive white markings on the head and legs, including the upper legs.
USES Riding; driving; show jumping.
HEIGHT About 15.2hh to 16.2hh.

Right Typical Gelderland features such as very flat quarters with high-set tail, convex profile, and large feet are shown here.

ANCESTRY

Many European breeds have been used in conjunction with native Gelder mares, with the addition of Eastern and Thoroughbred genes to create the modern, more refined Gelderland.

Friesian

The Friesian horse, or Harddraver, is at last being acknowledged as one of the original royal horses of Europe, although it is not as well known as its colleagues, the Andalusian, Lusitano, and Lipizzaner.

The horse hails from the coastal Friesland province of Holland, and its old name, Harddraver, means "good trotter" in Dutch. Coldblood horse remains from 3,000 years ago have been found in the area and prove the existence of similar ancestral horses from which the modern Friesian is descended.

The Friesian has spread throughout the world; its presence and active, showy trot in harness makes it very popular in show rings and in the festivals of its homeland.

Left The Friesian is now recognized as one of the old, original *Haute École* breeds. In Holland, it is also a much-loved carriage horse with remarkable trotting ability.

Left An excellent hack, the Friesian was also popular on farms, and was used in the formation of the German Oldenburg breed.

CHARACTER Most Friesians are quiet and sensitive, and can be fairly tractable.

PHYSIQUE The Friesian is a light to medium weight horse; compact and muscular with prominent withers; short, thick, well boned legs and hard feet; arched neck; powerful hindquarters; thick mane and tail.

FEATURES Friendly; gentle; regal; hardy.

COLOR Exclusively black with only a tiny white star permitted on the forehead.

USES Driving; riding.

HEIGHT 15hh or a little over.

ANCESTRY

Descended from the local primitive horse, the Fresian received Oriental and Adalusian crosses during the time of the Crusades. Cross breeding with the Oldenburg revived the breed in the early nineteenth century.

Schleswig Heavy Draft

A smallish heavy-type horse, the Schleswig Heavy Draft's status as a true heavy horse has often been contested due to its lack of height and cob-like character. The present breed was created to meet the demands for strong, fast draft power and, along with many other heavy draft breeds, was carefully bred for military and general heavy draft work.

Below Initially a rather heavy breed, the Schleswig Heavy Draft has been lightened and bred for more activity, and now, has a cob-like appearance.

CHARACTER The Schleswig has a lively temperament, and is a willing, hard worker.

PHYSIQUE A heavy cob-type horse; ears are of medium length, well pricked, and wide set; powerful shoulders; deep girth; compact body.

FEATURES Energetic; strong; good stamina.

COLOR Usually chestnut, particularly an attractive chocolate brown, with a wavy flaxen mane and tail, but bay and gray sometimes occur.

USES Heavy draft work.

HEIGHT From 15.1hh to 16.1hh.

ANCESTRY

Native heavy stock was mated extensively with Danish Jutland stock to produce the early Schleswig. Suffolk Punch, Cleveland Bay, and Yorkshire Coach Horse blood were used in the nineteenth century, with Thoroughbred additions. Most recently, Breton, Boulonnais, and once again, Jutland crosses have been introduced to the breed.

Westphalian

The modern Westphalian is yet another top-quality German horse which has been refined from an older version of the breed to produce the superior riding and competition horses required by today's market.

The Westphalian first came to the attention of the competitive horse world in 1978, when one of their number, Roman, won the World Show Jumping Championship. This intitial victory was followed by victories in jumping and dressage during the 1982 World Championships.

CHARACTER The Westphalian has a courageous, spirited temperament, yet is docile and willing.
PHYSIQUE A well-balanced, quality middleweight horse; moderately long ears; friendly eyes; straight profile.
FEATURES Strong; hardy; athletic.
COLOR All solid colors. White allowed on head and legs.
USES Riding; harness work; competition.
HEIGHT From 15.2hh to 16.2hh.

Right Bred for the modern performance horse market, the Westphalian contains fewer other breeds in its make-up than some warmbloods. It is a versatile horse, used for carriage driving, general riding, harness work, and especially show jumping and dressage.

ANCESTRY
Native Westphalian stock plus early Thoroughbred blood has been combined with Hanoverian, Arab, and modern Thoroughbred.

Swiss Warmblood

Switzerland's version of the warmblooded competition horse is based on its own ancestral breed, the Einsiedler, from the Swiss canton of Einsiedeln. According to Benedictine monks keeping records of local horse breeding in the eleventh century, the Einsiedler was a strong horse used for riding and driving.

In more recent centuries, Norman and Hackney blood was introduced into the Einsiedler and, later, Anglo-Norman blood as well. In the twentieth century, the Selle Francais and French Anglo-Arab were used. In the 1960s, Swedish, Hanoverian, Holsteiner, Trakehner, and Thoroughbred blood were brought in with the intention of creating a Swiss Warmblood able to compete on a world-class level.

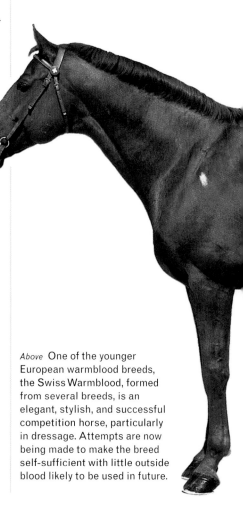

Above One of the younger European warmblood breeds, the Swiss Warmblood, formed from several breeds, is an elegant, stylish, and successful competition horse, particularly in dressage. Attempts are now being made to make the breed self-sufficient with little outside blood likely to be used in future.

CHARACTER The Swiss Warmblood has a docile, kind temperament and is a willing, cooperative worker.
PHYSIQUE An elegant quality horse; well-proportioned, attractive head; straight or slightly convex profile; ears of medium length; eyes, wide apart; sensitive muzzle with flaring nostrils.
FEATURES Free, supple gaits; good jumper; elegant.
COLOR All solid colors permitted, with white on the head and legs.
USES Riding; competition.
HEIGHT Averages at 16hh.

ANCESTRY

Based on old Einsiedler blood, several European breeds were introduced in the nineteenth and twentieth centuries to create a strong, athletic competition and general riding horse which could also be used in light harness.

Brabant

As selective breeding practices became popularized, the best horses for farming were considered those of immense size and muscle. Consequently, a variety of such breeds was developed, one of the most popular of these being the Belgian Draft horse, also known as the Brabant.

The Brabant hails from a Belgian crossroad which was traveled by a number of ancient heavy war horses. These animals are presumed to have contributed much to the Brabant, an ancient breed that has changed very little in appearance through the centuries, and which contributed much to the establishment of its fellow draft horses, including the Clydesdale and the Suffolk Punch.

At the breed's peak, almost all of Belgium's horses were Brabants. This changed with the dawn of twentieth century farm machinery in the fields, which rendered the steadfast farm horse virtually obsolete. Today, while it is viewed more as a meat animal than a farm hand in its homeland, the Brabant has found a rebirth in the United States where it has gained a devoted following for showing and farming purposes. It is enthusiastically received in the show ring, either in showing classes or in publicity displays. It is still used as a foundation stock in warmblood breeding.

CHARACTER The dominant characteristics of the Brabant are its docile temperament and its weight. It has been described as phlegmatic, even sluggish, but almost always good-natured. It is obedient, unflappable, reliable, and hard working.

PHYSIQUE Compact and massively muscled with short legs; short neck; broad back and chest.

FEATURES Very strong; enduring; hardy.

COLOR Most are chestnut or sorrel with flaxen manes and tails.

USES Heavy draft.

HEIGHT Ranges from 15.3hh to 17hh.

ANCESTRY

The Brabant's ancestor was the primitive Forest Horse of the Quaternary period, but more recently it is almost certainly descended from the Ardennes heavy horse and the Flanders/Flemish heavy horse.

Right The Brabant has a massively muscled body with an unmistakable impression of strength, weight, and power. This modern Brabant, with his lighter type and longer legs, takes after the Gris de Nivelles strain, showing good conformation and presence. He also shows a primitive coloring tendency to lighter under-parts.

Top left A Belgian Brabant fulfilling his original role as a working horse, in Colorado.

Breton

The Breton draft horse is a recently formed breed from Brittany in the northwest of France.

In the middle ages, the Crusaders' Oriental horses, brought back to France from the East, were introduced into the Brittany horse. This cross-bred two types of horse, the Sommier, and the Roussin.

Later, the Sommier and the Roussin were crossed with other breeds to create a heavier, stronger type of animal, now known as the Draft or Grand Breton.

CHARACTER The Breton has endurance and an amenable temperament.
PHYSIQUE Squarish and large head; heavy jaws; short, mobile ears; bright eyes; large and open nostrils.
FEATURES Powerful; active gaits.
COLOR Usually strawberry or red roan, but bay and gray also occur.
USES Light to heavy draft work.
HEIGHT 15hh to 16hh.

Below Both the Grand Breton and the lighter Postier-Breton are still used for work, with the larger Grand Breton also used for meat production.

ANCESTRY
Originally founded from small Asian heavy horses and local indigenous horses, later additions include Ardennais, Boulonnais, Percheron, Norfolk Roadster, and Hackney.

Norman Cob

The Norman horse was the basis for the Anglo-Norman, which has itself formed the progenitor base for riding and light harness horses. The Norman Cob was created in the seventeenth century specifically for riding, carriage work, and light draft work. Today, it is used as a light to medium draft horse.

Below The Norman Cob is still actively used as a working horse in France, mainly in agriculture and transportation.

CHARACTER Amenable, tractable, and energetic despite size.
PHYSIQUE Stocky but not coarse; proud head, held high; medium to short ears; broad forehead; bright eyes; small muzzle and nostrils.
FEATURES Tough; hardy; great stamina.
COLOR Chestnut, brown, and bay are the usual colors with occasional roans and grays.
USES Light to medium draft work.
HEIGHT From 15.3hh to as tall as 16.3hh.

ANCESTRY
Old Norman stock forms the basis of this unusual horse, with additions of Oriental and Norfolk Trotter blood.

Ardennais

The Ardennais originates from the Ardennes region on the borders of France and Belgium, but it is generally regarded as a French breed. It is one of the oldest breeds of heavy draft horses in the world, being directly descended from the prehistoric Diluvial Horse of Solutré. The Ardennais has never been a very tall horse and probably formed one of the base progenitor types for the mythic Great Horse of the knights of the Middle Ages.

The Ardennais has often been used as a cavalry horse, Napoleon having used them in his Russian campaign in 1812, where the breed survived the horrific Russian winter. In World War I, Ardennais were again used extensively, this time as artillery wheelers.

In the early nineteenth century, Thoroughbred and Arab blood were introduced into the breed, together with French Boulonnais and Percheron blood, resulting in variations within the breed. The three types of Ardennais now in existence are the original type of around 15hh which live in small numbers in the mountains; the Trait du Nord type, which is bigger, heavier, and more widespread; and the Auxois, a very heavy type probably containing less original Ardennais blood.

CHARACTER Unmistakably a heavy draft animal, the Ardennais has a primitive air to it, yet is tractable and easy to work with.

PHYSIQUE One of the heaviest, if not the tallest, types of draft horse; head can be quite light and finer than expected, with an alert expression; wide-apart ears; flat forehead; prominent eyes; straight profile.

FEATURES Hardy; energetic action; great strength.

COLOR A distinctive feature of the Ardennais is its very common strawberry roan color with black points. All other colors except black are accepted.

USES Heavy draft work; transportation; farm work.

HEIGHT From 15hh to 16hh.

ANCESTRY

Based on primitive indigenous stock, the Ardennais also contains Oriental and Thoroughbred blood with Brabant, Boulonnais, and Percheron infusions.

Left This example of the heavy draft Ardennais is not the usual strawberry roan, but more bay with just a hint of roan. Despite various other infusions, the Ardennais still retains an air of antiquity about it.

Camargue

The horses of the Camargue in south-eastern France spend much of their time in salt water, grazing on reeds and sparse coastal grasses until they are rounded-up each fall to select rising horses. Although they have lived and thrived in France for many thousands of years, they now number less than 500.

The Camargue horses are probably descendants of the primitive Diluvial Horse. During the nineteenth century, other blood was introduced by local horse breeders, although this seems to have had no lasting effect on the Camargue breed. However, culling of substandard colts and stallions has improved the breed.

Below No one seems to know just how long Camargue horses have inhabited the salt marshes of their homeland in south-eastern France. They are believed to descend from the primitive Diluvial Horse, but the shape of their heads seem to suggest a presence of Barb blood.

Above Today, the Camargue is used mainly for herding the wild black bulls of its homeland, which are often exported to Spain for bullfighting there.

CHARACTER Independent and spirited. Once broken in, the Camargue makes a docile and willing riding horse.

PHYSIQUE The tail is set low and, like the mane and forelock, is long and thick; sturdy and strong legs; extremely hard and well-formed feet; plain and big head; short, broad ears; pronounced, heavy jaws; expressive and wide eyes set well to the side of the broad forehead.

FEATURES Tough; hardy; enduring.

COLOR Almost always white-gray. Like the Lipizzaner, the foals are born dark but lighten with age. Bay and brown sometimes occur.

USES Trekking; herding; riding.

HEIGHT Around 13.1hh to 14.2hh.

ANCESTRY

Descended from the primitive French horse, the Camargue has undoubtedly received infusions of Barb and Arab blood centuries ago and, more recently, Thoroughbred, Arab, and French Postier-Breton, but to little effect.

Scandinavia

Norwegian Fjord

The color and markings of the Norwegian Fjord pony, along with the ancient tradition of mane-trimming, make it both unique and instantly recognizable in the equine world.

The Fjord has been known in Norway for thousands of years. The Vikings made full use of it in battle, as shown in the many carvings on Viking rune stones, employing the blood-thirsty practice of horse-fighting to select the best stallions for use and breeding.

Other northern European breeds of pony have Fjord blood in them, notably Britain's Highland Pony and the Icelandic Pony. They have also been exported to many European countries. The Fjord, or Vestland, as it is sometimes known, is very common throughout Scandinavia and appears in several similar varieties.

Right The Fjord's primitive markings, with an eel stripe from the poll to the tip of the tail and sometimes zebra marks on the legs, are remarkable.

Right The Fjord is still used for plowing on rough terrain, but is more popular as a trekking pony. It can also be seen in Fjord trotting races, long distance events, and competitive driving.

CHARACTER A true representation of the Celtic Pony group, the Fjord's coloring and markings are primitive. It has a kind, willing, and sometimes stubborn nature. It is very strong and tough, with good stamina.

PHYSIQUE Wide head; short and pointed ears, placed wide apart above a broad forehead; large, expressive eyes; open nostrils, but the muzzle sometimes has a stubby appearance; powerful body; concave profile; short neck; coarse upright mane; short legs with some feathering.

FEATURES Sure-footed; fearless; very hardy.

COLOR Distinct; nearly always yellow or cream-dun with a mane in three layers. Zebra marks often appear on the limbs. May have white on the head.

USES Farm work; driving; mountain work; pack horse; children's pony.

HEIGHT 13hh to 14.2hh.

ANCESTRY

Related to both Przewalski's Horse and the Tarpan, over the centuries the Fjord has received various inputs from other breeds, none of which were effective, and today it is regarded as purebred.

Icelandic Pony

Although Iceland has never boasted an indigenous pony, the well-known Icelandic Pony is the result of the interbreeding of many different strains and types descended from northern Europe's Celtic Pony. The ponies interbred freely, forming a hardy native animal, which was eventually recognized as a specific breed.

Below Icelandic stallions are selected for breeding based on the quality of their gait, one of which is the tølt, a very fast, comfortable running walk.

CHARACTER The Icelandic Pony requires almost no special care. It is quiet, inquisitive, friendly, and very independent.

PHYSIQUE Stocky build; short and thick neck; short and sturdy legs; short cannons; tough feet; large head; short, pricked ears; expressive eyes; long and full tail for cold-weather protection.

FEATURES Tough; hardy; has five gaits.

COLOR Almost any color can be found, and there are many variations and combinations.

USES Farm work; packhorse; draft; mining work.

HEIGHT From 12hh to 13.2hh.

ANCESTRY

The Icelandic Pony was brought by Norse and other settlers whose ponies contained different strains of the old Celtic Pony.

Knabstrup

The Knabstrup of Denmark is over 200 years old, and having gone from great popularity to near obscurity, is now swinging back into favor. As often happens when a horse is bred for color, the Knabstrup had by the nineteenth century deteriorated, becoming coarse, disproportionate, with differing types developing within the one breed. The breed eventually developed into a strong, plain harness type which is now known for its characteristic spotted coat. Recently, the addition of Thoroughbred blood has resulted in a much improved animal.

CHARACTER A quality riding horse, the Knabstrup is intelligent, perceptive, tractable, and easy to handle.
PHYSIQUE Head set onto the neck with a noticeable arch to the clean throat; pricked ears; friendly and intelligent eyes; straight profile; squarish muzzle with sensitive open nostrils.
FEATURES Solid and dependable; active; comfortable riding horse.
COLOR A wide variety of different spots and splashes on a white or roan coat. Some, however, still show the all-over spotting of the old Knabstrup. The mane and tail are sparse.
USES Riding; circus.
HEIGHT Between 15.2hh and 15.3hh.

ANCESTRY
The old breed was based on Fredericksborg and Iberian blood. Today, Thoroughbred blood is now being used to upgrade the breed.

Right Formerly a victim of breeding almost entirely for eye-catching color and markings, the Knabstrup is now bred more judiciously and makes a good middle-weight riding horse.

Swedish Warmblood

Swedish Warmblood indigenous stock was derived from the northern coldblooded pony and horse types. When in the seventeenth century a superior type of cavalry horse was required, the Royal Stud at Flyinge began to cross the native stock with a wide variety of other European breeds, including Iberian, Friesian, Arabs, and Barbs.

This process continued for many generations, and as time went on, the breed was refined with later additions of Hanoverian, Trakehner, English Thoroughbred, and selected Arab blood. Today, the breed is self-sufficient and is still bred at Flyinge.

The Swedish Warmblood is now one of the most successful competition horses in the world and has repeatedly won Olympic medals in the three disciplines of dressage, eventing, and show jumping. It is also a superb competitive carriage-driving horse.

Right Formerly a superior cavalry horse, the Swedish Warmblood is today one of the most successful competition horses in the world. It is one of the few warmbloods fast enough for eventing.

CHARACTER Swedish Warmbloods are tractable and intelligent. They have excellent jumping ability and flowing, elastic gaits.

PHYSIQUE Alert expression; long ears; alert, bold eyes; straight profile; long, crested neck, well muscled and set on long, sloping shoulders; long and well-muscled legs; strong and well-formed feet.

FEATURES Fast; great stamina for horse trials.

COLOR Most colors, but black is rare.

USES Riding; competitions.

HEIGHT Usually 16.1hh to 17hh, but quite a few animals are smaller.

ANCESTRY

Indigenous Swedish pony and horse types were initially mated with Iberian, Friesian, Arab, and Barb stallions. In the twentieth century, Thoroughbred, Hanoverian, and Trakehner blood was introduced for further refinement of the breed.

Gotland

The Gotland, or Skogruss pony is one of the most ancient breeds in the world. Along with the Bosnian, the Konik, and the Huçul, it is a direct descendant of the original wild Tarpan, and still shares many of its physical characteristics.

Below Exportation of the popular Gotland pony in the 1950s caused a dramatic fall in the native population. Government action was taken in an attempt to increase depleted numbers. It now thrives as a riding and performance pony, and also competes in trotting races.

CHARACTER The Gotland is an attractive pony, possessing much of its native resilience. Some have a strong independent, stubborn streak, however most are tractable and willing.

PHYSIQUE The tail, mane, and forelock are long and full; fine legs that are well muscled with good joints and strong tendons; tough, small, well-shaped feet; small head; broad, pricked ears; wide forehead; large eyes; straight profile.

FEATURES Good jumpers; strong; good stamina.

COLOR The most common colors are black and bay. Many have an eel stripe down the spine.

USES Trotting races; children's pony; harness work.

HEIGHT 12hh to 13.1hh.

ANCESTRY

An ancient breed descended from the Tarpan containing small amounts of Oriental blood.

Northlands

The Northlands pony is little known outside its homeland of Norway. It belongs to the North European type of prehistoric Celtic Pony and closely resembles the Scottish Shetland Pony.

Until the 1920s, this pony was used and bred by Norwegian farmers. No particular selection policies were followed, but the pony remained completely purebred.

By the 1940s, however, numbers had fallen to a mere 43, but a particularly fine stallion named Rimfakse, reinstated the breed from an almost certain extinction. Today, it is mainly used as a children's pony.

CHARACTER The Northlands is quiet-natured, but energetic. It is strong and tough, requiring only minimal care to keep it in good health and condition.
PHYSIQUE Well-proportioned, slightly large head; short, pricked ears; large eyes; straight profile; rather small nostrils; strong sturdy legs that are well muscled with well-formed joints; small, tough feet.
FEATURES Requires frugal keep; fairly impervious to bad weather.
COLOR Chestnut, gray, bay, and brown. No significant white.
USES Farm work; children's pony.
HEIGHT Around 13.2hh to 14.2hh.

ANCESTRY

The indigenous pony of Norway, the Northlands belongs to the Tarpan bloodline of the Celtic Pony group.

Right This kind-natured, willing, and active pony is popular as a children's mount and as a farm worker on ground too difficult for machinery.

Finnish

The Finnish, or Finnish Universal, is a coldblooded heavy horse. It was developed from native Finnish ponies which were then crossed with other breeds. Originally both light and heavy strains existed, but only the light type exists now. The Finns traditionally bred horses on the basis of performance rather than appearance. Hence, the Finnish is known for its speed, stamina, and agility.

CHARACTER Finnish horses are quiet and tractable, lively and intelligent. They are strong and willing workers.
PHYSIQUE Chunky build; square and heavy head; short neck; upright shoulders; deep chest; long back and strong hindquarters; strong legs with light feathering.
FEATURES Tough; fast; long-lived.
COLOR Chestnut is the most common color. Bay, brown, and black are also found.
USES Farm work; riding; trotting.
HEIGHT Between 16hh and 17hh.

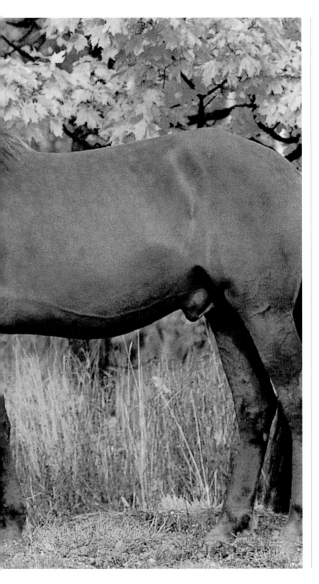

ANCESTRY

Indigenous Swedish pony and horse types were initially mated with Iberian, Friesian, Arab, and Barb stallions. In the twentieth century, Thoroughbred, Hanoverian, and Trakehner blood was introduced for further refinement of the breed.

Left The Finnish was formerly bred in both heavy and lighter types. Today the lighter type performs as a racing trotter.

Dole-Gudbrandsdal

The Dole-Gudbrandsdal is very similar to the British Dales Pony, and it is likely that they stem from the same prehistoric ancestor. The Dole-Gudbrandsdal comes in varying but recognizable types within the breed, partially because it is a dual breed (the Dole and Gudbrandsdal were originally separate breeds which have now become amalgamated), but also because other types of blood have been introduced into it — from heavy draft blood to trotting, Thoroughbred, and Arab blood — making it a versatile breed capable of different tasks.

CHARACTER Patient, kind temperament combined with great stamina. Requires minimal care. Subsists on meager feed.

PHYSIQUE Head can be heavy and Roman-nosed, or lighter with a straight profile; short and mobile ears; gentle eyes; open nostrils.

FEATURES Energetic; very strong; great stamina.

COLOR Mainly black and brown with some bay. Palomino and gray also occur though more rarely.

USES Trotting races; farm work; forestry; harness.

HEIGHT From 14.2hh to 15.1hh.

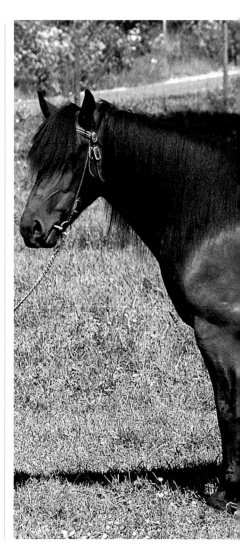

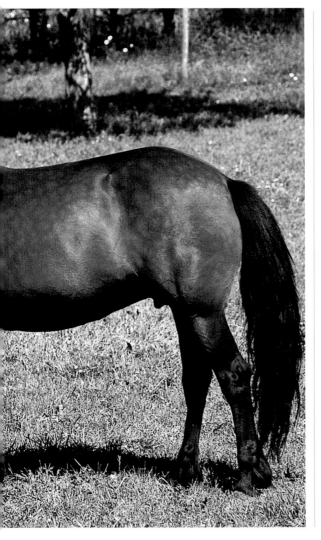

ANCESTRY

Belonging to the Celtic
Pony group, there is almost
certainly Friesian blood
present, with other additions to
create different types within the
dual breed.

Left A combination of two
breeds, the Dole and the
Gudbrandsdal, this breed
has also had infusions of
other breeds. An offshoot of
the breed, the result of
extensive Thoroughbred
crosses, is the Dole Trottez.

Danish Warmblood

The Danish Warmblood, along with the Swedish, the Hanoverian, and the Dutch, is one of the world's premier warmbloods. Monasteries often seem to have taken particular interest in breeding horses, and the Cistercian monks, in what is now Holstein, bred horses from the early fourteenth century, putting mares of large German breeds (such as the old Holsteiner) to high-quality old Iberian stallions. However, Danish access to German horse breeds only lasted until Holstein was seized by Prussia in 1864.

The great Royal Fredericksborg Stud was founded mainly on the Neapolitan and Andalusian breeds, near Copenhagen in 1562, but Denmark's native small coldblood horse and also the larger Jutland carthorse were also mated with Iberian, Dutch, Turk, and later, Thoroughbred stallions. However, in order to create a suitable twentieth century competition horse from their largely Fredericksborg-Thoroughbred mares, the Danes selected Anglo-Norman, Thoroughbred, Trakehner, Wielkopolski, and Malapolski stallions for breeding. In warmblood breeding, the Hanoverian was not usually used.

CHARACTER Danish Warmblood horses are hugely successful at the highest level of equestrian competition, particularly in dressage and show jumping. Their temperament is almost always equable and willing, yet they possess spirit, courage, and individuality.

PHYSIQUE Substantial yet refined build; virtually perfect legs, well-muscled in their upper parts; big, clean joints; excellent, well-made feet; longish and fine ears; generous and expressive eyes.

FEATURES Supple, elastic, and flowing, graceful action.

COLOR All solid colors, bay being most common. Some white is permitted on head and legs.

USES Riding; show jumping.

HEIGHT Consistently between 16.1hh and 16.2hh.

ANCESTRY

Over the centuries German and Danish mares were mated with Iberian, Neapolitan, Dutch, and Turk horses. The Dutch Warmblood was created by breeding the resulting mares with Thoroughbred, Trakehner, Anglo-Norman, Wielkopolski, and Malapolski stallions.

Left One of the few European warmblood breeds with no Hanoverian blood, the Danish Warmblood nevertheless contains many warmblood and Oriental genes. These have created a hugely successful competition and performance horse in the modern continental European mold.

Frederiksborg

Today, when we talk about *Haute École* horses, we mention Lipizzaners, Lusitanos, and Andalusians. In fact, when *Haute École* was at the height of its popularity in the nineteenth century, the Frederiksborg was one of the most popular horses used in its disciplines.

Unfortunately, the Danes could not resist the demand from other countries, and unwisely sold too many of their prime breeding stock, thus depleting the stock significantly.

A few of the old-type Frederiksborgs remained in Denmark, nurtured by private breeders, but it was not until about 75 years later that Frederiksborgs began to reappear and be registered once again in the stud book. The breed had to be bred up again, with Oldenburg, Friesian, Thoroughbred, and Arab blood.

CHARACTER The Frederiksborg is plain, but strong and agile with an equable temperament.
PHYSIQUE Substantial, but fairly short neck set and carried high on a deep, broad chest; rather long legs, but well set and strong; readily pricked ears; particularly good trot; friendly eyes.
FEATURES Quality carriage horse; good stamina; fast; agile.
COLOR Almost always chestnut.
USES Riding; medium draft work.
HEIGHT From 15.lhh to 16.lhh.

ANCESTRY
The Royal Frederiksborg Stud began with Neapolitan and Iberian stallions used on native Danish, Jutland, and Holsteiner mares. Old Iberian, Dutch, Turk, and early Thoroughbred stallion blood made up the original Frederiksborg. Today's Frederiksborg was revived with Oldenburg, Friesian, Thoroughbred, and Arab blood. Thoroughbred blood is continuing to be infused.

Above The old type of Frederiksborg was a *Haute École* horse par excellence. The modern version, shown here, is primarily a carriage horse, but increasing infusion Thoroughbred blood will, in time, make it into a competition warmblood.

Southern Europe

Skyros
Italian Heavy Draft
Lusitano
Salerno
Andalusian
Altér Real

Skyros

The smallest and best known of Greece's indigenous breeds is the Skyros. This pony, named after a Greek island, is also probably one of the purest breeds in the world. It resembles the ancient Tarpan breed, which suggests that it is a direct descendant.

The Skyros has little substance and poor front conformation. It is mainly used for fetching water and carrying packs, though it is also ridden sometimes. However, when kept in better conditions, this breed improves considerably in strength and appearance.

Right The little Skyros of Greece has a tough life, eking out a hardworking existence on poor keep.

CHARACTER The Skyros is willing and has an amiable temperament. It is also a very hard worker.
PHYSIQUE Small head and ears; short neck; upright shoulders; narrow body; long legs with tendency toward cow hocks.
COLOR Dun, brown, or gray.
USES Excellent packhorse; light farm work; children's pony.
HEIGHT 9.1hh to 11hh.

ANCESTRY
The Skyros is believed to be related to the Tarpan.

Italian Heavy Draft

The Italian Heavy Draft is a relatively new breed. The Italians were never inclined to breed massive, phlegmatic horses, so when they produced their own heavy draft, they bred a small animal with lively action and bright temperament. It is a newish breed, having only been developed in 1860.

CHARACTER The Italian Heavy Draft has a friendly, calm nature, although some are notably highly strung.
PHYSIQUE Fine and small head; small, pricked ears; broad forehead; lively eyes; short, strong neck; flaring nostrils; full mane; short and sturdy legs with strong joints.
FEATURES Tough; hardy; easy to care for.
COLOR Many chestnuts, with flaxen, full mane, forelock, and tail. Red roan and bay also occur. Distinctive coat shadings and patterns in many of the solid-colored horses occur.
USES Although some are still used in agriculture, the breed's main use today is as a meat animal.
HEIGHT 14.2hh – 16hh.

Below Though undoubtedly a heavy horse, the Italian Heavy Draft has a lively nature and plenty of personality. The breed is active, energetic with compact strength.

ANCESTRY

Local native stock was mated initially with Arab, Hackney, and English Thoroughbred, with later introductions of Brabant, Boulormais, Ardennais, and Percheron. Postier-Breton was used extensively.

Lusitano

The Lusitano, like the Andalusian, is descended from the old Iberian saddle horse. Named after its country of origin (Lusitania was the Roman name for Portugal), the Lusitano's name came into use as a description of Portugal's Iberian horses in the early twentieth century. The name was officially adopted in 1966.

The Lusitano is bred mainly in the agricultural heartland of Portugal, and the fertile south and west around the River Tagus, for participation in the *corrida*, or bullfight. In Portugal, the bull is not killed, the whole fight takes place on horseback, and it is a major disgrace if the horse is injured. The horses are highly prized, painstakingly schooled, and are the epitome of agility, courage, and grace. Their temperament is spirited, willing, and cooperative.

In addition, the stallions are normally schooled to the highest standards of *Haute École* before being sent out to stud. The Lusitano is a late-maturing but long-lived breed, and is generally not broken in until at least three and a half years of age.

CHARACTER The Lusitano is a proud, gentle, nimble, and extremely well-balanced horse. It is most courageous, and willing and obedient by nature.
PHYSIQUE Small head and ears; almond-shaped and alert eyes; open and mobile nostrils; rounded, tapering muzzle; muscular neck; powerful hindquarters; compact body; hard, round, and small feet; long, fine legs; abundant mane and tail.
COLOR Gray, brown, bay, and chestnut are the most common colors.
USES Bullfighting; farm work.
HEIGHT 15hh to 16hh.

ANCESTRY

Like the other Iberian breeds, the Lusitano is based on the primitive Sorraia pony, which still exists in the peninsula. In the past, some Oriental blood was also introduced.

Above The Lusitano was one of the favored
royal horses of Europe, with its traditional
rounded outline, sloping croup, and gently
convex profile. Never bred in the same
numbers as its blood-brother, the Spanish
Andalusian, it is used more for work, than a
parade or display mount.

Salerno

Italy has long been a horse-breeding country. By the twentieth century, it was a leading producer of some of the best racing Thoroughbreds, largely through Federico Tesio, who bred such world-beaters as Ribot and Nearco. Another Federico, this time Caprilli, was the innovator of the forward seat for the Italian cavalry, which has become the basis of modern jumping and cross-country riding. Caprilli must have therefore been very familiar with the Salerno, which was used extensively as a cavalry horse in the twentieth century.

The Salerno was developed by heavily infusing the Neapolitan with Andalusian blood and other Oriental strains. The breed was favored by King Charles III of Naples, and later of Spain, but internal unrest in the country meant that in 1874 the Salerno's special breeding program ended.

The Salerno was established in its modern form by the middle of the twentieth century.

Left The head and facial expression reveal the elegance and spirit expected of an Italian breed. Some Salernos need tactful handling, but most are cooperative and even-tempered.

CHARACTER The Salerno is spirited and lively, but has a level nature. Some Salernos need tactful handling, but most are cooperative and even-tempered.

PHYSIQUE Elegant head; broad forehead; longish ears; alert eyes; flaring nostrils; hard legs; strong feet.

COLOR Any solid color. White permitted on legs and head.

USES Leisure riding; competition.

HEIGHT Around 16.1hh.

ANCESTRY

Originally of old Neapolitan stock, today's Salerno looks nothing like its Iberian forebears. This is due to copious infusions of Arab and Thoroughbred blood.

Left The Salerno was established in its modern form by the middle of the twentieth century. It was a favored mount of the Italian cavalry for the sports of cross-country riding and show jumping.

Andalusian

The modern Andalusian is probably amongst the purest and oldest breeds in the world.

Along with its blood-brothers, the Lusitano, Carthusian, Altér Real, Castilian, Extremeño, and Zapatero, the Andalusian represents almost exactly the type of horse depicted in Iberian prehistoric cave art. Iberia was a noted horse-breeding area during its time as a Roman province, when Arab, Barb, and other Oriental strains were brought there. Many thousands of years before that, it contained horses of typical Spanish or Iberian type — high-headed, convex profile, compact, strong build and high action, proud, and gentle.

The Andalusian is a major world breed, which has influenced many others and is very highly prized in Spain. It was taken to the Americas by the conquistadores, and has influenced American and many European breeds. As a warhorse, it had all the qualities needed to perform the battlefield manoeuvers necessary for a knight's mount. The peak of its systematic breeding stretched from the fifteenth to the eighteenth centuries.

To introduce height and more weight, heavier stallions were used, which almost decimated the breed's prized qualities of fire and pride with docility, and contaminated its compact conformation and proud action.

CHARACTER Pride, courage, and spirit combined with docility and affection toward people, typify the Andalusian's character.

PHYSIQUE Powerful, crested neck; laid-back shoulders; broad and deep chest; sturdy with a straight, fairly short back; wavy mane and tail; strong and muscular loins and quarters; elegant, strong legs with short cannons.

COLOR Gray (predominantly), bay, auburn-brown, some chestnut and roan.

USES Display; bullfighting.

HEIGHT 15.1hh to 15.3hh.

ANCESTRY

The native Spanish horse, Ginete, and the native ponies, Garrano and the Sorraia, mated with Barbs and Arabs to produce this lovely Andalusian.

Left Shown here is an Andalusian of the older type, with his rounded outline and powerful hindquarters.

Right An Andalusian of the more modern type, lighter and with longer legs, but still showing that old nobility, which made the breed such a huge favorite in the bullrings and classical riding schools of Europe centuries ago.

Altér Real

The Altér Real is the second of Portugal's aristocratic *Haute École* and bullfighting horses, but unfortunately it suffered in Napoleon's Peninsular Wars much more than its brothers, the Lusitano and Andalusian.

The Altér Real was founded on the blood of 300 Andalusian mares imported from Jerez by the Portuguese royal house of Braganza. This established a stud in the Alentejo province specifically to provide the royal court in Lisbon with good *Haute École* and carriage horses. The stud was later moved to the small town of Altér do Chao, which subsequently gave the horse its name, Real, meaning "royal" in Portuguese.

Breeding was successful, and the Altér Real thrived until the Peninsular Wars, when the stud was ransacked and the best horses stolen by Napoleon's troops. Later, efforts to reinstate the Altér Real by the introduction of English Thoroughbred, Hanoverian, Norman, and Arab blood led to the weakening of the breed's type and character. In the early twentieth century, when the Portuguese monarchy was abolished, the breed's stud records were destroyed and the stock dispersed.

Today, the Altér Real owes its thriving existence to Dr. Ruy d'Andrade. An expert breeder of the true Iberian horse, he built up a top-quality stud of Altér Real horses, which he passed to the Portuguese Ministry of Agriculture. The breed has since been owned by the state.

CHARACTER Intelligent, hardy, responsive, fiery, and spirited.
PHYSIQUE Substantial and arched neck; powerfully muscled upper legs; thrusting hocks.
COLOR Nearly always gray, but also bay, black, and chestnut.
USES Riding; light draft work; mainly for *Haute École* displays.
HEIGHT 15hh to 16hh.

ANCESTRY
The Altér Real was bred from the Andalusian breed of horses during the eighteenth century.

Above Due to unsuitable infusions in the past, the temperament of some Altér Reals is somewhat excitable, and therefore, the breed sometimes requires skilled handling.

Eastern Europe and Central Asia

Shagya Arab

Mezöhegyes, the oldest stud in Hungary, is the home of the Shagya Arab. In 1816 a military edict ensured that the broodmares at Babolna be cross-bred with Oriental stallions to provide light cavalry and harness horses.

The results following the edict were so satisfactory that a generation later it was decided that Babolna should focus on producing horses of exclusively Arab blood. These became the forerunners of today's Shagya.

CHARACTER Shagyas are intelligent, spirited yet gentle, and enthusiastic.
PHYSIQUE Mane, forelock, and tail are of long, straight, and silky hair; wide-set, pointed ears; large eyes; broad, domed forehead; small muzzle with flaring nostrils; arch to the throat.
FEATURES Hardy; frugal; active.
COLOR Most Shagyas inherit their founding father's satiny gray coat, but all Arab colors can be found, including the rare black, inherited from "The Black Pearl of Hungary," the perfect stallion O'Bajan XIII (foaled in 1949), at stud in Babolna.
USES riding; light driving; cavalry.
HEIGHT From 14.2hh to 15.2hh.

Right A riding horse of the highest quality, the Hungarian Shagya deserves international recognition.

ANCESTRY

Based on indigenous Hungarian mares but with Oriental infusions, the Shagya is a high-quality horse of marked Arab type.

Nonius

Following Napoleon's defeat at Leipzig in 1813, the Hungarian cavalry captured the Anglo-Norman stallion, Nonius Senior, from the French stud Rosières. Nonius Senior's sire, Orion, was apparently not full Thoroughbred, but a halfbred, the other half probably being Norfolk Roadster.

Nonius Senior had several significant faults such as poor hindquarters, a long, weak back, a short neck, and big ears.

Below A popular and generally useful breed, all Nonius horses to this day look extremely like their founding stallion.

CHARACTER The Nonius is a calm, easy-to-handle horse.
PHYSIQUE Long and plain head; moderately long ears; big, generous eyes; straight or slightly convex profile; honest, friendly expression.
FEATURES Strong; long-lived.
COLOR Black, dark brown, or bay. Sometimes a little white on head and lower legs is seen.
USES Riding; farm work; light draft work.
HEIGHT The large Nonius stands between 15.3hh and 16.2hh, while the small Nonius stands between 14.2hh and 15.3hh.

ANCESTRY
The founding sire was of Anglo-Norman and Norfolk Roadster blood. The founding mares were Arab, Andalusian, Lipizzaner, Norman, and Kladruber breeds, with some English halfbreds. Later, Thoroughbred and Arab blood was introduced.

Furioso

The Furioso, or Furioso North Star, may have a slightly strange name, but, like other Hungarian breeds, it takes its name from the stallion who founded it. The Hungarians like quality, responsive, and intelligent horses, and the middle-weight Furioso shows all these qualities.

CHARACTER The Furioso is intelligent with a cooperative and pleasant temperament.

PHYSIQUE Pleasing, proud appearance; Thoroughbred-like head; medium length ears; long, strong neck; straight profile; squarish muzzle; large, open nostrils.

FEATURES Robust; coach-horse type of action; excellent carriage horse; great strength and stamina.

COLOR Brown, bay, or black. Very rarely carries any white.

USES Riding; driving; competition; steeple-chasing.

HEIGHT Averages at around 16.1hh.

Below In view of the type of competition horses currently in demand, the Furioso continues to receive infusions of carefully selected Thoroughbred blood.

ANCESTRY

English stallions of Thoroughbred and Norfolk Roadster blood were used on mares of Nonius and Arab blood. Thoroughbred genes were reintroduced in the nineteenth century and are still being used today.

Murakosi

The Murakosi, or Murakoz, is a Hungarian energetic draft and agricultural horse, which was developed during the early twentieth century. It is now bred in two types — one light and one heavy. Both have a strong, robust physique. Until World War II, the Murakosi was immensely popular, but due to decimation during the war and the decline in demand, its numbers are now much reduced.

Below The Murakoz is bred in two types — a large, heavy type and a lighter, but still draft type.

CHARACTER The Murakosi is kind, willing, and docile.
PHYSIQUE Large head with convex profile; strong frame with pronounced dip in back; powerful hindquarters; muscular legs with light feathering.
FEATURES Strong; active.
COLOR Bay, brown, black, gray, or chestnut, with flaxen mane, tail and feather.
USES Draft; farm work.
HEIGHT 16hh.

ANCESTRY
The breed was developed by crossing Brabant, Ardennais, Percheron, and Noriker blood with native animals.

Malopolski

The Malopolski, or Polish Anglo-Arab, is another horse created by the skillful and horse-loving Poles to meet modern demands for a quality riding and competition horse.

The Malopolski comes from the same progenitor base as its now fairly distant relative, the Welkopolski, containing Masuren and Poznan blood.

Below The Malopolski, or polish Anglo-Arab, is a substantial Thoroughbred.

CHARACTER The Malopolski is courageous, spirited, and energetic, yet it has a calm and even temperament.
PHYSIQUE Arabic in general appearance; high-set tail; long legs; well-proportioned head with a slight dish; medium-length active ears; broad forehead; eyes set well down and to the side; muzzle tapers to flaring nostrils.
FEATURES Great stamina; good jumper; good carriage horse.
COLOR All solid colors including roan.
USES Riding; competition.
HEIGHT From 15.3hh to 16.2hh.

ANCESTRY
The Malopolski is based on native stock with considerable infusions of Thoroughbred, Arab, and Anglo-Arab blood.

Huçul

The Polish Huçul (or Huzul) pony is closely related to the Konik Pony. The homeland of the Huçul is the Carpathian mountain range in the south of the country, and the pony is often called the Carpathian Pony. Unlike the Konik, it has been infused with generous amounts of Arab blood, so does not closely resemble the original wild type.

Below The Huçul is descended from the wild Tarpan, but contains more native pony blood than its close relation, the Konik, and a good deal of Arab blood.

CHARACTER The Huçul is said to be fearless, and is willing to work. It is also very docile.
PHYSIQUE Full mane and tail; smooth and high action; a short, wedge-shaped head; snub muzzle; straight profile; small, pointed ears; small eyes.
FEATURES Tough; hardy.
COLOR Usually bay or light chestnut with flaxen mane and tail, but duns and grays also occur.
USES Children's pony; farm work.
HEIGHT 12hh to 13hh.

ANCESTRY

Descended from the Tarpan, the Huçul contains some native pony blood and a great deal of Arab blood.

Konik Pony

The Polish Konik Pony is much closer to its ancestors than other ponies. The word "konik" means "little horse" in Polish and does not denote a specific breed, as there are five various strains. The type normally referred to as the formal Konik breed is believed to have descended from the original wild Tarpan of Eastern Europe, which was an Oriental type of small horse with a fine head and the primitive markings of a dorsal stripe and zebra markings on the legs.

Below Poland's Konik pony is a direct descendant from the wild Tarpan. It has been used to re-establish the now extinct Tarpan breed.

CHARACTER Late-maturing but very long-lived. Although most are easy to handle, some retain the wild streak of the Tarpan and may be independent and difficult.

PHYSIQUE Long, well-shaped, muscular neck; long, generous mane; strong, pony type legs; small, tough feet with a little feathering; heavy head; short, pricked pony ears; small muzzle with flaring nostrils.

FEATURES Hardy; tough.

COLOR Mostly gray or dun, both often with a bluish tinge, and bay. There is a dark dorsal stripe and sometimes zebra markings on the legs.

USES Farm work; children's pony.

HEIGHT From 12.3hh to 13.3hh.

ANCESTRY

The Konik is believed to contain a large amount of original Tarpan blood, with some Arab and other local infusions.

Wielkopolski

The Wielkopolski has a short history, having only been bred after World War II. Closely related to the Trakehner, it is mainly based on indigenous Polish and Eastern European stock, crossed with Arab, Thoroughbred, and West European strains. Its native content includes two Polish warmblood horses, the Masuren and the Poznan. Both of these are no longer formally recognized by the Polish, although limited numbers live alongside the Wielkopolski.

CHARACTER The Wielkopolski is a middle-weight with a gentle temperament. It is intelligent, quiet, and hard-working.

PHYSIQUE Workman-like; moderately long ears; expressive, lively eyes; medium-width forehead; open nostrils; straight profile.

FEATURES Sturdy; good stamina; good carriage horse.

COLOR Usually chestnut or bay.

USES Light draft work; riding; competition.

HEIGHT From 16hh to 16.2hh.

Below The Wielkopolski was developed in Poland after World War II, and is one of the youngest breeds in the world.

ANCESTRY

The Wielkopolski is a true representative of its part of the world, containing both Eastern and Western European strains with a strong reliance on its native regional breeds.

Don

The Don comes from the area around the rivers, Don and Volga, on the bleak Russian Steppes where the Cossacks came from. Indeed, the Don was the Cossacks' mount. It was a small, exceptionally tough and wiry horse, highly independent with incredible stamina, and seemingly impervious to the vicious Russian winter. It descended from the indigenous Steppe horse, which ran free in the Caucasus Mountains, appearing to thrive on whatever food it could forage.

Below The Don was the horse of the Cossack cavalry that made history in the war with Napoleon. He disastrously underestimated both the merciless Russian winter and the sheer toughness of the Don horses. Independent, tough, and strong, the Don is still used for endurance riding.

Above These days the Don is mainly used for endurance riding, for which it is admirably suited.

CHARACTER The modern Don has an independent character. It is bred in large numbers in the Steppes, where it can run free and needs little care from humans.

PHYSIQUE Long neck; long broad back; smallish, shapely, and pricked ears; large and expressive eyes; straight profile; open nostrils; short and somewhat jarring action; strong hindquarters; long hard legs.

FEATURES Tough; strong; versatile; frugal.

COLOR Usually brown or chestnut but bay, black, and gray sometimes occur. There is often a metallic sheen to the coat.

USES Pleasure riding; endurance riding; racing.

HEIGHT Between 15.2hh to 15.3hh.

ANCESTRY

Indigenous Steppe horses were mated with various Asian and Oriental strains to create the earlier type of Don associated with the Cossacks. Later, Orlov, Thoroughbred, and Strelets Arab blood was added.

Vladimir Heavy Draft

The Vladimir Heavy Draft was developed in Russia after the Russian Revolution. Developed from British and French heavy horses, the Vladimir has a strong physique. It was registered as a breed in 1946, and is suited to heavy draft work.

Below Although the breed is heavy, it has a majestic air and upstanding posture.

CHARACTER The Vladimir Heavy Draft is docile, good-tempered, and active.

PHYSIQUE Small head; long strong neck; powerful shoulders; broad body; stout hindquarters; strong legs with feathering.

FEATURES Active; powerful.

COLOR Bay is most common, but it also comes in chestnut, brown, or black.

USES Heavy draft work; farm work; transportation.

HEIGHT Between 15.2hh and 16hh.

ANCESTRY

The Vladimir was developed by crossing Cleveland Bay, Suffolk Punch, Ardennais, Clydesdale, Percheron and Shire.

Budyonny

The Budyonny, Budenny, or Budyonovsky horse is one of the newer Russian breeds, created after the Russian Revolution. One of the people's heroes of the Revolution was Marshal Budyonny, whose aim was to create the perfect cavalry horse. It had to have stamina, toughness, an equable temperament, courage, and physical prowess involving both speed and jumping ability. The military stud farm at Rostov was chosen as the location for the development of the breed, which was to be named after its instigator, Marshal Budyonny.

CHARACTER The Budyonny is a kind-natured, patient, intelligent horse, but it has, nevertheless, spirit, courage, and enthusiasm.

PHYSIQUE The head shows definite Thoroughbred ancestry; long sloping shoulders; strong compact body; straight or slightly concave profile; open and flaring nostrils.

FEATURES Speed; stamina; jumping ability; hardy; tough.

COLOR Most Budyonnys are chestnut, or bay with a golden sheen.

USES Endurance riding; racing.

Right The Thoroughbred quality of the modern Budyonny is clearly seen in this horse. Intended as the perfect cavalry mount, the Budyonny today is a high-quality competition horse.

ANCESTRY

Thoroughbred stallions on Don mares are the main foundation of this breed, with additions of Kazakh, Kirgiz, and Chernomor blood.

Orlov Trotter

The Orlov Trotter was founded in 1777 by Count Alexei Grigorievich Orlov, Commander of the Russian fleet during the reign of Catherine the Great. Count Orlov defeated the Turkish fleet at Chesme in 1770, and was presented by the Turkish admiral with an Arab stallion, Smetanka.

Smetanka had one season at the Orlov Stud and left only a handful of progeny from Danish, Dutch Harddraver, Mecklenburg, English Thoroughbred, and Arab mares. But the following year a Danish mare foaled a very moderate colt named Polkan. He was cross-bred with a Danish mare, and the result was an outstanding trotting stallion named Bars I, regarded as the founding father of the Orlov Trotter.

Bars I was cross-bred with a variety of mares — Arabs, Dutch, Danish, English halfbreds, Polish, Russian, and Mecklenburg and their crosses — breeding selectively for quality, strength, stamina, and trotting ability. The Orlov Trotter is now one of the fastest trotting breeds in the world.

CHARACTER The Orlov Trotter is active and bold.
PHYSIQUE Small head on long neck; upright shoulders; broad chest; deep girth; straight back; powerful loins and muscular hinquarters.
FEATURES Strong; tough; active; fast.
COLOR Mostly gray, but black and bay also occur.
USES Trotting; driving; riding.
HEIGHT Quite varied in range, from 15.2hh to 17hh.

ANCESTRY

An Arab base with a variety of European breeds, with modern infusions of American Standardbred.

Left The Orlov Trotter was the fastest trotting racer in the world before the advent of the Standardbred, and still provides entertainment in Russia.

Left This brown gelding shows the short front, upright shoulder, and long, sturdy legs typical of harness racers.

Métis Trotter

Early in the twentieth century, the Russians realized that their world-famous, record-breaking, and hitherto invincible racing trotter, the Orlov, was being beaten hands down by the American Standardbred. Accustomed to being the best in the world, the Russians refused to admit defeat. Instead, they purchased a number of American Standardbreds and cross-bred them with their beloved Orlovs. The result was a new breed of faster trotter, known as the Russian or Métis Trotter.

Sadly, despite nearly a hundred years of crossing and selective breeding using the very best trotting blood from both the Standardbred and the Orlov, the Métis Trotter is still not as fast as the Standardbred, although it is faster than the pure Orlov. In 1949, the Métis Trotter was recognized as a breed in its own right.

CHARACTER The Métis Trotter is an even-natured horse, renown for being energetic, and courageous.

PHYSIQUE Resembles a tough, quality halfbred with powerful, sometimes croup-high hindquarters; fairly straight neck; well-balanced physique; trotting action exhibits dishing in both the forelegs and hindlegs; forelegs are slightly knockkneed and the hindlegs, cow-hocked; moderately long, well-shaped ears; small eyes; straight or slightly convex profile. The head is not as fine as one might expect.

FEATURES Fast; good stamina.

COLOR All solid colors are present in the breed.

USES Racing — this horse was specifically bred for racing at a fast trot.

HEIGHT Between 15.1hh and 15.3hh.

Above With its powerful, straight shoulders, high croup, and long legs, this horse is unmistakably a fast harness racer bred to rival the Standardbred. It contains many of its genes, plus those of the famous Orlov Trotter. Its speed currently falls between those two breeds.

ANCESTRY

The Métis Trotter is a straight cross between the Orlov Trotter and American Standardbred.

Tersky

The modern Tersky was created early in the twentieth century as an Arab-type horse for military use. The old-type Tersky horse was used by the Cossacks because it was tough and enduring. In the twentieth century Marshal Budyonny refined the breed by adding more Kabardin, Don, Arab, and Thoroughbred blood.

There are three types of horse within the breed: a light, fine, Arab-looking type; a more substantial intermediate type; and a thicker-set type with sturdier legs and a longer body.

CHARACTER The Tersky has a gentle yet spirited temperament, and is very intelligent.
PHYSIQUE Straight profile; deep chest; muscular hindquarters; fine hard legs; high-set tail.
FEATURES Good stamina; excellent jumping ability; fast.
COLOR Gray with a metallic silver sheen. Can also be bay.
USES Flat racing; competition; circus.
HEIGHT Not a tall horse, between 14.3hh and 15.1hh.

ANCESTRY

Native Ukrainian mares and indigenous old-type Terskys were initially put to the Strelets Arab. Later, Kabardin, Don, Arab, and Thoroughbred blood was used to refine the breed.

Left The strong Arab character of the modern Tersky is obvious in this beautiful horse. As well as this Arab type, there are two other types of Tersky. They are all excellent performance horses.

Kabardin

The Kabardin originally came from the North Caucasus Mountains, where it was an old and established breed. It is a strange mix, with Oriental characteristics such as being fine skinned with long, mobile ears and open nostrils, and traits of those horses native to the colder climes of the North Caucasus Mountains.

Kabardins are very popular in their homeland, the Republic of Kabardin-Balkar, and are bred at two main studs in their native country where they are then used for transportation and riding purposes. They are also bred and used extensively in neighboring states, where they are used as sports horses, as well as in the development of other breeds. Extremely fertile, they are also used to produce milk.

As a mountain horse, the Kabardin is sure-footed, nimble, sensible, and intelligent enough to pick its own way to find a safe route. It also has great stamina and can work in snow and in deep, fast-flowing water.

CHARACTER The Kabardin has a willing temperament, and is sensible and intelligent.
PHYSIQUE Oriental in appearance; smooth and comfortable action; long head; slightly convex profile; pronounced jaws; long ears with inward-turning points, set close together; small eyes; open nostrils.
FEATURES Sure-footed; strong; enduring; nimble.
COLOR Bay, brown, black, and occasionally gray, but never white.
USES Riding; transportation; good sports horse.
HEIGHT Between 14.2hh and 15.1hh.

ANCESTRY

The Kabardin is descended from the wild Tarpan, and in the early twentieth century, Karabakh, Turkinene, Persian, and Arab strains were infused into the local indigenous stock.

Left The Kabardin is said to be the safest and most reliable mountain horse in the world. An unusual mixture of Oriental and colderblooded features combine to create great stamina and hardiness in this breed.

Ukrainian Riding Horse

The Ukrainian Riding Horse was founded after World War II. The original purpose for this new breed was to create a high-class riding and competition horse, which was successfully achieved. The colts begin work very young, at just 18 months, and are tested for individual talent and aptitude in racing, dressage, show jumping, and cross-country. The best are normally kept for breeding.

CHARACTER The Ukrainian Riding Horse has a good temperament. It is kind-natured, obliging, and a willing worker.

PHYSIQUE Elegant and refined in appearance; head is occasionally rather large; straight profile; pricked ears; alert eyes; open nostrils.

FEATURES Strong; good stamina; good carriage horse.

COLOR Usually chestnut, but bay and black are also found.

USES Riding; competition; light harness work; farm work.

HEIGHT Up to 16.1hh.

ANCESTRY

Local native mares, Nonius, Furioso North Star, and Gidran mares were cross-bred with Trakelmer, Hanoverian, and Thoroughbred stallions to produce this breed.

Left **A young breed developed as a quality performance horse after World War II, the Ukrainian Riding Horse is also used for light harness work and in agriculture. It regularly represents the Ukraine in competitive events.**

Latvian

The Latvian probably descended from the prehistoric, heavy draft Forest Horse of Northern Europe. Some experts, however, believe it is based on a tough and spirited pony indigenous to Lithuania, the Zemaituka (based on Tarpan and Arab blood).

The Latvian now occurs in three types, due to the different breeds introduced into it — the heavy type, the Latvian Draft; a standard or intermediate type, the Latvian Harness Horse; and a lighter type, the Latvian Riding Horse.

The Draft is the original type from which the others have been developed. It has more substance and strength, and can be used as a heavyweight riding horse. The Latvian Harness Horse was developed in the 1920s by infusing Hanoverian blood into some strains; others received Anglo-Norman, Oldenburg, and Norfolk Roadster blood to create a slightly heavier type. Both types are used for riding and competition.

The Latvian Riding Horse, a more recent development, contains substantial crosses of Thoroughbred and Arab blood, and often resembles a warmblood trotting horse.

CHARACTER Latvians have a quiet, relaxed temperament.

PHYSIQUE Rather long and proud head; straight profile; small, pointed ears; large, gentle eyes; big nostrils; a full mane and forelock.

FEATURES Strong; has a great deal of stamina.

COLOR Black, brown, bay, chestnut, and occasionally gray.

USES Riding; competition; farm work.

HEIGHT Between 15.lhh and 16hh.

ANCESTRY

Descended from the Northern Europe Forest Horse and the Tarpan/Arab-based Zemaituka pony. Three types now exist due to varying infusions of Finnish Heavy Draft, Swedish Ardennes, Hanoverian, Oldenburg, Norfolk Roadster, Thoroughbred, and Arab blood.

Left The Latvian is a stronger breed than its appearance would indicate. Developed for about 300 years mainly as a draft animal, there are now, due to the mingling of other breeds, draft, harness, and heavyweight riding types. All combine a quiet temperament with strength and stamina.

Karabakh

The Karabakh horse comes from the Karabakh Mountains of Azerbaijan, and is of pony size. It has an Arab-like appearance, which isn't surprising as both horses come from the same genetic type.

The Karabakh's existence was documented as far back as the fourth century, and it has remained popular ever since as a riding mount. In the eighteenth century, it was suddenly very much in demand and was exported to many other Asian and European countries.

Today, it is said that no pure Karabakhs are left because in the past the breed was diluted by Persian, Turkmene, and Arab blood. They are used largely as racing and riding horses.

CHARACTER The Karabakh is a spirited and refined hotblood horse. It is beautiful, calm, and gentle. Like all true mountain breeds, it is sensible with an innate sense of direction.

PHYSIQUE Refined and small; long legs, often ending in blue-black feet; quite small oriental type head; straight profile; pointed ears; large eyes; soft, fine muzzle.

FEATURES Surefooted; tough; energetic.

COLOR Like some other Russian breeds, the Karabakh has a beautiful metallic golden sheen to its coat. Usually golden dun with black points, often with a dark eel stripe down its spine. Some white markings may occur. Other colors are chestnut, bay, and gray.

USES Riding; racing.

HEIGHT Around 14.1hh.

ANCESTRY

An ancient hotblood type, the Karabakh has been mixed with Persian, Turkmene, and Arab blood.

Left The long legs, spare frame, and high-set, sparse tail declare this horse's Oriental genes. A small mountain horse, its talents include racing, pack work, and mounted games.

Akhal-Teké

The Akhal-Teké from Turkmenistan is the living descendant of the now-extinct old type of Turkmene horse, and is very highly regarded in its home country. It is known to have existed in its present type around 3,000 years ago, when it was used as a fast warhorse. Evolved and reared in varying climates from searing heat to killing cold, the breed is one of the hardiest and most enduring in the world.

Historically, the Akhal-Teké is a true desert horse, coming from an arid region with vast expanses of steppe and desert. Although they did (and still do) run in herds under the management of a mounted herdsman, today many are still traditionally tethered and hand-fed barley, eggs, alfalfa, mutton fat, and a fried heavy type of bread when they are needed for work. Heavy covers were used to protect these fine-skinned horses, both from the bitter nights and daytime desert sun. In the past, foals were weaned at two months, and yearlings were raced hard.

Left Akhal-Tekés are high-class riding horses: they race, jump, and take part in endurance and dressage competitions. They are a premier sports horse in Turkmenistan, Russia, and other Eastern countries.

ANCESTRY

Belonging to the old Turkmene group of horses, the Akhal-Teké has influenced and helped found many breeds, including the Thoroughbred.

CHARACTER Noted for being stubborn, rebellious, somewhat wild, independent, bad-tempered, and occasionally vicious.

PHYSIQUE Offbeat conformation; long, narrow neck, carried very high; pronounced withers; very big, sloping, and narrow shoulders; shallow, narrow, and rounded body; fine legs that are too long for the body; a truly aristocratic head, which is fine, long, and lean; wide-set and beautifully chiseled ears; wide, flat forehead; large, bold eyes; straight profile; widely flaring nostrils.

FEATURES Highly enduring; magnificent movement.

COLOR Bay, gray, chestnut, and black occur, but the most highly prized color is the honey-golden dun with black points. The coat has a peculiar and strong metallic sheen.

USES Riding; competition.

HEIGHT 15.2hh, though looks bigger.

Right The conformation of the Akhal-Teké is being changed, to some extent, by selective breeding for the modern competition horse market. This horse looks more like a modern Thoroughbred.

Bashkir

The Bashkir, or Bashkirsky, has been bred on the southern slopes of the Ural Mountains in Russia by the Bashkiri people for many centuries. They use it for pulling sleighs and troikas, and for making *kumiss*, an alcoholic liqueur, made from the mares' milk.

The most remarkable feature of the Bashkir is its long, thick, wavy winter coat. A common variant is tight curls, like Persian lamb, and the most startling of all are tight ringlets up to about 6in (15cm) in length. The summer coat is short and straight.

There are about 1,200 Bashkir "Curlies" (as they are called) in the United States, where they clean the horse in winter by vacuuming it! The Bashkiri people use the body, mane, and tail hair for spinning textiles and making clothing.

CHARACTER Bashkirs are kind, affectionate, and very willing workers.
PHYSIQUE Stocky; distinct cold-climate features; big, heavy head; very short and pricked ears; gentle, intelligent eyes, set wide apart; a straight profile; small but open nostrils; short legs; tail held close to hinquarters.
FEATURES Tough; hardy; enduring.
COLOR Usually bay, chestnut, or palomino, and quite a few have Appaloosa markings.
USES Endurance riding; transportation; harness.
HEIGHT Around 14hh.

ANCESTRY

The pure Bashkir seems to be an indigenous ancient type in itself, with typical cold-climate features. In recent times some other breeds have been crossed into it to bring size and quality.

Left The Bashkir is famous for its long, curly winter coat, a vital necessity in its cold home climate in the Ural Mountains. However, in the summer their coat is short and straight, as seen here.

Kladruber

The Kladruber of Bohemia, in the former Czechoslovakia, was founded in 1597 by the Emperor Maximilian II of Austria. It was bred as a ceremonial coach horse for the Imperial Austrian court of Vienna.

In the Kladruber's formative years, the breed was the subject of very careful selective breeding, and animals were specifically bred as parade or coach horses. The horses were mainly gray, but some blacks were also bred.

World War II ravaged the Kladruber stocks. To revive the breed, Anglo-Normans, Hanoverians, and Oldenburgs were cross-bred with existing Kladrubers, and the breed thrived once again.

CHARACTER The Kladruber is calm and amenable by nature.
PHYSIQUE Deep and muscular neck; strong legs with broad, flat joints; very little hair on the fetlocks; medium-sized, well-formed feet; a classical look to the head indicating its origins; moderately long ears; large eyes; broad forehead; open nostrils.
FEATURES Strong; enduring; active.
COLOR Almost always gray, but blacks are still bred.
USES Riding; driving; draft work.
HEIGHT In the past Kladrubers were 18hh, but today's representatives of the breed are about 16.2hh to 17hh.

ANCESTRY

Alpine mares were bred with Barb and Turk stallions. Later, Andalusian, Lipizzaner, and Neapolitan blood was introduced. In this century, Anglo-Norman, Hanoverian, and Oldenburg blood was used to revive the breed's numbers.

Left This historic coach breed is held in great affection. An impressive, distinctive type of horse, the Kladruber contains, on its native heavy base, much old Spanish blood, only receiving crosses of other breeds after World War II.

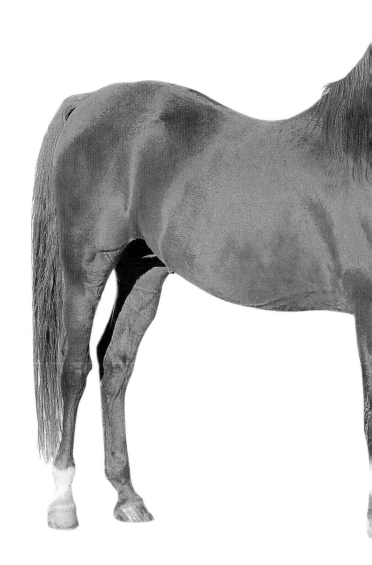

Middle East
and Africa

Arab

Caspian

Barb

Arab

The Arabian or Arab sprung from the deserts of the Middle East thousands of years ago. The circumstances surrounding its true origins will always remain a mystery — folklore suggests Biblical, Islamic, and even supernatural involvement — but there is no denying the spell that this beautiful desert breed has always cast upon the human species. Few horses harbor such great affection as the Arabian.

Though today it is one of the best-known, most beautiful, and athletically gifted breeds in the world, the Arabian has remained the world's best kept secret, living among the nomadic Arabs who first cultivated and cherished the breed as their most valued possession. Over time, word of the Arabian spread beyond the borders of its homeland, and newcomers instantly recognized its gifts. What startles many who first encounter the Arabian is that in addition to possessing great beauty, it is also the quintessential equine athlete. Centuries of selective breeding in the desert have resulted in a versatile horse known for its talents in all equine activities.

The Arabian is the oldest purebred in the world, and is considered a national treasure in nations as diverse as England, the United States, Egypt, Hungary, Poland, and Russia. Indeed, the pedigree of almost every horse on our planet today has been influenced in one way or another by the ageless Arabian.

Left The Arab is often described as "dish-faced," as a concave outline to the front of the face is desirable. Eyes are often large and expressive and set wide apart.

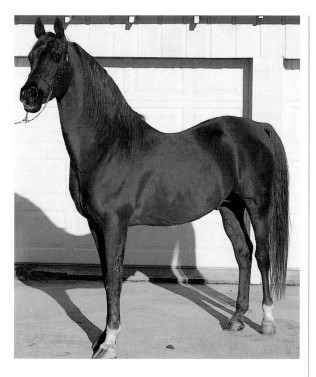

ANCESTRY

The modern breed we now call the Arab seems to have fewer infusions of other types than most other breeds. Its introduction to Arabia is relatively recent, stemming from the time of Mohammed, for there is no evidence of native Arab stock before that time. Realizing their value as a war weapon, Mohammed imported horses from other Middle Eastern countries in large numbers and encouraged their breeding and improvement.

CHARACTER The Arabian is undoubtedly beautiful and versatile. Though hotblooded it is also very affectionate.

PHYSIQUE Long neck; short back; sloped shoulders; deep chest; muscular legs; prominent withers; good bones; dished face; wide forehead, large nostrils and eyes.

COLOR Most solid colors with dark skin; gray and black are popular.

USES Riding; endurance; light driving; racing.

HEIGHT 14.1hh to 15.1hh.

Above Almost every horse breed in the world today has been influenced by the Arab. Breeding programs have been designed in England, The United States, Egypt, Hungary, Poland, and Russia to ensure that the quality of the Arab never diminishes.

Caspian

The Caspian should be regarded as a small horse rather than a pony because it has horse rather than pony characteristics. Remarkably, despite having been domesticated, it seems to have descended in pure form from an Oriental prehistoric horse, the fossils of which have been found in Iran and match the Caspian's skeletal features. One of the best depictions of this ancient horse can be found on the seal of Darius the Great, ruler of Persia in 500 BCE.

All theories pointed to the horse's extinction around the tenth century, but in 1965, forty Caspians were discovered in a remote area of the Elburz Mountains in Iran by Mrs. Louise Firouz, who shipped them to Britain. It is now claimed that the Caspian is the oldest purebreed in the world.

Left The Caspian is now thriving in studs in Britain, the United States, Australia, New Zealand, and Iran.

CHARACTER Alert yet equable and of affectionate temperament.

PHYSIQUE The Caspian is a miniature Oriental type, with a free, floating action. A miniature Thoroughbred head; short and pricked ears; wide and domed forehead; large, bold, and intelligent eyes; straight profile; low-set nostrils that are readily flared; arched, strong, and elegant neck; long, full, and silky forelock, mane, and tail hair; fine and strong legs; exceptionally hard feet which do not need shoeing.

FEATURES Narrow; responsive; intelligent; gentle; cooperative.

COLOR Bay, gray, and chestnut, rarely black or cream.

USES Riding; driving; beginners' pony.

HEIGHT Between 10hh and 12hh.

ANCESTRY

As a direct descendant of the primitive type, the Caspian is a piece of living prehistory with no known infusions of other blood. It is claimed to be the progenitor of the Arab.

Left One of the equine success stories of the twentieth century, the ancient Caspian, having been believed extinct for about 1,000 years, was rediscovered in Iran in 1965.

Barb

The Barb, or Berber, is one of the old Oriental-type breeds which has, over many centuries, greatly influenced other breeds as well as found many of the most successful breeds of the world today. Along with the Arab, its place in equestrian history cannot be denied. Yet, it is little known and has not achieved worldwide popularity like the Arab. It does not even share the status of other lesser-known Oriental types such as the Akhal-Teké and the Turkoman.

The Barb's original homeland is North Africa — Morocco, Algeria, Libya, and Tunisia. Today, it is bred at a large stud at Constantine in Algeria, and at the stud of the King of Morocco. The Tuareg people and some of the nomadic tribes of the remote mountain and desert areas of the region, probably still breed a few Barb-type horses.

CHARACTER Temperament is not as equable or affectionate as that of the Arab, to which it is invariably compared; also not as spirited or as beautiful as the Arab and does not have its springy, action but is exceptionally tough and hardy.

PHYSIQUE Lightly built; strong and arched neck of medium length; fine but tough legs; extremely hard and well formed hoofs; profuse mane and tail hair; long and narrow head; fine and pointed ears; slightly convex profile; low-set and open nostrils.

FEATURES Enduring; fast; responsive.

COLOR True Barbs are black, bay, and dark bay/brown. Those with Arab blood show other colors.

USES Riding; racing; display.

HEIGHT From 14.2hh to 15.2hh.

ANCESTRY

Possibly from primitive European rather than Asian stock, the Barb is a hotblood Oriental type infused with a good deal of Arab blood.

Left The Barb is one of the pervading Eastern influences on most of today's horse breeds, particularly old Iberian stock which founded most of the American breeds.

Far East and Australia

Java Pony
Przewalski's Horse
Sumba
Australian Stock Horse
Australian Pony

Java Pony

The Java Pony is also known as the Kumingan Pony. In its native Java, this little pony pulls the *sados*, or two-wheeled taxis, and over the centuries has therefore adapted to hard work in a tropical climate. Similar breeds are to be found on other Indonesian islands: the Timor (of delicate build), the Bali (a primitive breed used as a packhorse), the Batak and Gayoc from Sumatra, and the Sandalwood (a fast pony from Sumba). The Java Pony is similar to the Timor, but it is bigger and stronger with a better conformation. This is due to the Arab influence.

CHARACTER The Java Pony is of a quiet disposition. It is willing to learn, industrious, and very easy to handle.
PHYSIQUE Slightly built but strong pony-type; small oblong head; long ears; expressive eyes; narrow yet muscular neck; sloping shoulders; deep and wide chest; long back; sloping croup; high-set tail; light but strong legs; hard and tough feet.
FEATURES Strong; good stamina.
COLOR Most colors.
USES Riding; driving; all-round work pony.
HEIGHT Stands at about 12.2hh.

ANCESTRY

Primitive Asiatic Wild Horse and Tarpan cross breeds infused with Arab and Barb blood.

Left This Java Pony has had the benefit of Arab blood, which makes it bigger and stronger than others in this region. It is a "taxi" pony on Java and is also used for riding and other light draft work.

Przewalski's Horse

As far as the modern Western world is concerned, Przewalski's Horse, or the Mongolian or Asiatic Wild Horse, was discovered in 1881 by the Polish explorer, Colonel N. M. Przewalski. He had been given a skull and the skin of a three-year-old animal by the chief magistrate of Zaisan, who had obtained it from some hunters who discovered the remains in the Gobi Desert in western Mongolia. Colonel Przewalski presented the remains to the Zoological Museum of St. Petersburg in Russia, where the naturalist I. S. Poliakoff examined them and pronounced that they belonged to a distinct species of wild horse.

Today, we know that the Przewalski has almost certainly been hunted to extinction in the wild, as no sightings of it have been made since the 1970s. However, a captive population is being built up from animals caught in the wild earlier, and reintroductions are being made into Russia, China, and France. There are also several herds in zoos and parks around the world, and breeding is very carefully controlled through the stud book held at Prague Zoo.

Top Right Almost hunted to extinction, reintroduction of this breed to the wild, notably in Russia, Mongolia, and China, with a thriving population in France, is meeting with some success. The Przewalski's Horse is showing its inherent adaptability by acclimatizing to whatever region it finds itself in.

Left All the Przewalski's Horse herds are considered feral rather than wild.

CHARACTER They are aggressive and afraid of man, yet the stallions are courageous in defending their herds, particularly when foals are present.

PHYSIQUE Very stocky; short and thick neck; reasonably long back; fine legs; elongated and tough feet; coarse and heavy head; no forelock; fairly small eyes, set high up the head; convex or straight profile; small and tight muzzle with small, low-set nostrils.

FEATURES Ferocious temperament when annoyed or disturbed; tough; frugal; great stamina; fast over short distances.

COLOR Yellow dun is the most common, but coat color ranges from red dun to creamy dun. The horses have a dark dorsal list or stripe, often with zebra markings on the legs. The lower legs are black. The mane and tail are black. The muzzle and eyes are surrounded by oatmeal-colored hair.

USES Not used or tamed by man; zoo exhibits.

HEIGHT From 12hh to 14h.

ANCESTRY

Today's Przewalskis are direct descendants of their primitive ancestors.

Sumba

The Sumba Pony, also called the Sumbawa Pony, comes from the islands of Sumba and Sumbawa. It bears a close resemblance to the Mongolian and Chinese ponies. This pony is widely used for a variety of jobs from light draft work to riding. However, it is best known as a dancing pony and is used for equestrian "dancing" competitions throughout Indonesia. In these competitions, the ponies wear bells on their knees and dance to a tom-tom rhythm, with young boys riding them bareback. Due to its extraordinary strength, the Sumba Pony is also used in the game of lance throwing.

CHARACTER Sumba ponies are quiet and willing workers. They are very industrious, intelligent, and tough.

PHYSIQUE Primitive pony type with a large heavy head; upright mane; sparse tail; upright shoulder; deep chest; straight back; sloping croup; flat withers; fine but strong legs; well-formed hoofs.

FEATURES Specializes as dancing pony; tough; hardy; fast; agile.

COLOR Dun with dorsal stripe and dark points.

USES Dancing; all-round work pony.

HEIGHT 12.2 hh.

ANCESTRY

A cross between a Mongolian Wild Horse and Tarpan. Later, Dutch colonists infused Arab blood to improve the breed.

Left Probably closely related to the Mongolian and Chinese ponies, the Sumba shows primitive coloring and markings with a large head.

Australian Stock Horse

The most prominent of Australia's horses today is the Australian Stock Horse, an animal developed for working the vast herds of livestock on the country's rugged terrain. But the Stock Horse's story actually begins with that of another breed: the Waler, a horse of profound endurance, strength, jumping ability, and intelligence. While this horse was originally bred to work the outback sheep stations, it soon gained a reputation as a military horse. It served in many conflicts away from its home territory; more than 100,000 were used in World War I alone. By the end of World War II, its population greatly declined and the Waler virtually faded away.

The Waler's legacy inspired a group of horsemen in the 1970s to establish the Australian Stock Horse Society, through which a fine line of Australian horses would be bred and preserved.

Above This Australian Stock Horse shows much Quarter Horse character but with obvious Thoroughbred influence.

CHARACTER The Australian Stock Horse has good temperament, courage, toughness, and stamina.

PHYSIQUE Medium to long neck; sloped shoulders; slightly sloped croup; strong back; good legs; powerful hindquarters; good muscle overall.

COLORS All colors permitted, with white allowed on head and legs. Bay is most common.

USES Herding; rodeos; riding; competition.

HEIGHT Approximately 14.2hh to 16hh.

ANCESTRY

A considerable mixture of old European stock with some Asian and Arab genes. Additional Barb and Thoroughbred infusions make up the present-day Australian Stock Horse.

Left The breed has had a fairly checkered history in its short lifetime, but is now established and popular in many spheres, being used for general riding, stock work, rodeos, and as a competition horse.

Australian Pony

Australia's children, like children everywhere, wanted their own ponies. Although ponies had been imported with horses during the settlement years, it was not until the late nineteenth century that any effort was put into developing a set type. A recognizable type emerged by the early 1920s, and a stud book was started shortly afterward.

Above The Australian Pony is a mixture of pony blood from Europe and Indonesia, plus the Eastern influence of the Arab and Thoroughbred. It is popular as a trail, and endurance pony, as well as children's riding pony. It also goes well under harness.

CHARACTER The Australian Pony is an excellent riding pony, refined yet not too light. It is renowned for being sound and healthy, robust, responsive, and even-natured. It shows its "blood" ancestry, but does not require cosseting, and it is easy for children to ride and care for.

PHYSIQUE Arab-like head; short, pricked ears set well apart; broad forehead with wide-set, large and generous eyes; straight or slightly concave profile; tapering muzzle and flared nostrils; well-shaped neck, attractively arched with a full mane; fairly fine legs, long and strong in their upper parts; short cannons; tough tendons; hard, well-shaped feet.

FEATURES Excellent temperament; elegant; enduring; athletic; hardy.

COLOR Gray is very common, but any color is permissible with the exception of parti-colors. White on head and legs is allowed.

USES Suitable children's riding pony; endurance riding; harness.

HEIGHT From 12hh to 14hh.

ANCESTRY

Very mixed, including various European breeds, in particular Shetland, Welsh, and Exmoor.

Index